From:
Grandpa
Keith

Function
By Default

[signature]

Keith Simpson

"2012"

Exitus Ex Obscurum Press

Function By Default
©2011 Keith Simpson. All rights reserved.

First published March 2011

Exitus Ex Obscurum Press
3116 E. Shea Blvd, Suite #165
Phoenix, AZ 85028

www.functionbydefault.com

Printed in the United States of America

ISBN: 978-0615460376

Book and cover design by The Concentrium
www.theconcentrium.com

Library of Congress Control Number: 2011923413

DEDICATION

This book is dedicated to those of us who are not satisfied with what we've been told and must search deeper. To those who cannot quench their thirst for knowledge. To the children who in their purity should know these things before life gets going too fast. To those not pure of mind or heart who may find an alternative in the information presented here. Finally, to you, the reader, for your interest.

In memory of Lester and Lorena Simpson who did a good job with what they knew. My elders, who taught me not to accept only the obvious.

A special thanks and gratitude to Bill Burton, Eddie Sutterth, Charlie Hill, and Charlie Douglas; my 12-Step sponsors without whom I might have quit long ago.

To all my children who may not have gotten what they deserved; and Maris for giving me Shane, and a safe place to heal and begin this journey.

There is a principle which is a bar against all information, which is proof against all arguments and which cannot fail to keep a man in everlasting ignorance — that principle is contempt prior to investigation.

Herbert Spencer

CONTENTS

Phase 4: Re-unification / Willingness

Phase 5: New Education / Change

Phase 6: Sponsorship / Sharing

† Words marked with this symbol are defined in the Glossary

Life on the Knife

*In my time I've seen, more than my
share of good and bad lives*

*Love has become just a varying degree
of the spectrum of pain*

*Life has no meaning when you won't
acknowledge what you've become*

*Tomorrows and yesterdays all seem the
same when they're gone*

*Now it's time to stop denying yourself
and look at reality*

Survival is balanced, ever precariously

On the edge of a knife

In the darkness beyond.

Keith Simpson
"1982"

PREFACE

I'm an addict—

And when my addictions reared their ugly head, I had no recourse, but to be swept into an eddy of self centered self-destruction, loathing and hatred. Not only was I swept away, I enjoyed the ride. It wasn't a terrifying journey; it was "The Hunt." I liked this detachment from reality. "It" was my life. I sought the feeling with everything that was in me. Time, people, places and things mattered little. I was on a run; I was consumed. Fear and ego are strange bedfellows. As Ross Perot Once said, "like a giant sucking sound—."

Thank you for reading this. It was not written to glorify me, or addiction of any kind. Let me take this moment to apologize to all the people who got hurt just being in my vicinity. Especially, let me never forget the children, wives, and the elderly whom I disregarded. To the people who ran with me, and those who understand this concept — you should have moved.

Life became a consequence. The life I chose was denial. Denial created a void. The void became a vacuum. To fill this vacuum I poured in drugs, money, women, adrenalin and fantasy. It became insatiable. It was addiction. When addiction became my reality, I had no control. As a kid I was grabbed by the nape of my neck by teachers, parents and cops on a regular basis. This type of control never worked. They could force me to go where they wanted me to be, but they couldn't make me stay. Addiction didn't grab me, it shackled, manacled, strait-jacketed and thumb screwed me. It plunged me into the depths of the deepest sea and dared me to breathe, flung me naked onto the arctic tundra and taunted my trembling. When it got bored of torturing me, it abandoned me helpless, broken and battered on the steps of a 12 step program — what a long strange trip it was.

Life has become a journey of discovery[†]. I have often felt as though I was dropped into a parallel universe by mistake. Everything appears to be seen in a mirror; crystal clear, but in reverse. It only makes sense in hindsight, if at all. Whether it makes sense or not is irrelevant. It is reality. I'm here — so I may as well participate.

Keith Simpson

INTRODUCTION

Recovering from a dysfunctional lifestyle cannot occur while in a vacuum or holding pattern. Escaping a vacuum is difficult at least. Being drawn back into destructive relations or situations is very common. It may not feel good or right, it just feels familiar. Venturing into the unknown without an experienced guide is a fear few can overcome. A different living environment or relationship may be conducive† to change but repeating behaviors in a new location or situation seldom changes the outcome. This is a holding pattern of dysfunction. Without an expansion of awareness we are destined to mirror our past pain. We become empowered to change our present beliefs, feelings, and values when we accept and begin to implement† new truths. Without change, growth is doubtful.

Growth is progress, not maintenance or tolerance. The goal and gift of this modality is to provide to the participant a new road, a new road to a different and more functional destination. Understandable, visible, obtainable relief is made available. Those requiring, or seeking, these changes, need to take the actions. Presenting new information† and assistance in its implementation† requires knowledge of this action†. The structure of this modality is such that there is measurable progress in each phase. As new information is understood and experimented with, a pattern of change emerges. As resources expand, so do the options for a more functional future. This progress is most apparent to the participant. It is their recovery†, or change that is, after all, most important.

This program is a multi-level modality. Achieving change is done by the implementation† of a six-phase program which is both progressive and measurable. The topics presented in each of the six phases are strategic to the corresponding level of growth or change. Some participants may proceed at a faster or slower rate than others. The program is not time sensitive or demanding. It is strictly based on growth and development. The success of the program is in the hands of the participant, as is their future.

PHASE 1
Information

Information[†] is the communication of facts and knowledge. This being the first of six phases is to expose facts that may have never been learned, taught or considered. This is an intelligence gathering phase where a person may learn new information. Consideration and investigation is hoped for. If this level of participation is accomplished, the choices are but three: 1) This information is accepted and implemented[†] 2) It is rejected and any truth it contains is denied 3) Something presented here may be retained for future integration[†] or sharing[†].

The intent of this phase is to clarify facts to oneself, not require compliance but rather to inspire change. It is hoped that the motivation for reading this is to glean[†] some sort of insight into life, or that of another. If it's for your personal information, it is hoped that the current state of your life will be enhanced and expanded by this "new information" and that you may prosper and grow as a result of it.

The goal of the first phase is to encourage the participant to admit the current facts that are present in their life. Developing an understanding that, living is more than existing, growth is more than aging, and happiness is not continuous. In the course of doing the research of phase one, it is hoped that this new information will instill a desire to pursue even more new types of views and information to enhance life. A decision to proceed will be of benefit not only today, but for the rest of life.

PHASE 2
Implementation

Implementation[†] is the performance of a task. This challenge is not to be an event, but rather a new outlook on life. To implement[†] this outlook into life requires practice. Life skills are developed through practice, much the same as destructive behaviors are developed over time. No one magically wakes up one morning and is someone other than who they fell asleep as, they develop into that person over a period of time. This development could have resulted from dedication and hard work with loving teachers and capable role models. It could also be a result of pain or fear and was developed as a means of survival. No matter how one becomes what they are is not so much fate, as conditioning and repetition.

Discovery[†] is the core fundamental, or intent, of this phase. After knowledge is amassed, implementation[†] is required to practice and hone the new information for one's benefit. Often major obstacles block the use of this information. "If nothing changes, nothing changes" was never truer than in recovery[†] from any disfunction. If things don't take on a new light or meaning, old behaviors and beliefs seem to remain. Some of what had worked in the past has to be evaluated to determine if it impedes future progress.

The goals of phase two are organization of facts leading up to the present, facing them in a manner that is understandable, validating our participation in the events as they occurred and the realization that bad choices do not make bad people. New information allows new choices which allow for new outcomes and consequences.

PHASE 3
Action

Action requires decision and effort. Without decision there is no commitment, and without commitment there can be no long standing change. Effort is required to break old habits both in behavior as well as thinking. Action is a choice[†]. Change may be the result of the choice. A belief must develop in oneself that life may improve if these changes occur.

The intent of phase three is to instill a desire to change. "If" the choice is made to broaden one's base of knowledge by taking this action, improvement or at least change, will begin. Time is required to hone these new skills. Time was required to develop the problems we face today. It is hoped that at this phase in the program, one would be willing to accept their part in their own dysfunction. By doing so, they open the door to change and improvement. Functional boundaries are established and values are understood.

The goal of this course of action, or decision, is that it be willful. Coercion would defeat the purpose of holding one accountable to see the process through. Total implementation[†] is necessary in order to overcome the obstacles which will surely present themselves. It is important at this time to present viable[†] alternatives to old behaviors and attitudes.

PHASE 4
Re-Unification

Reunification[†] implies[†] a return to wholeness. At times everyone has felt incomplete. Some have never had the luxury of feeling whole. Others have lost it through events that may or may not be of their own doing. Wholeness is a key element in a human being. Balance is the key ingredient to wholeness. Honesty and personal responsibility are the means to achieving it.

Instilling a desire and willingness to proceed is the intent of this phase. Balance of the past, the present and the foreseeable future through information and acceptance are stressed. Fear, in its many forms, is explored and understood. Its history in a person's life is examined and faced. Freedom from the control of fear, guilt and shame are considered. Lines are drawn to separate fear from what it is and what we thought it was.

Goals in this phase are that the attendee begin to resolve past issues that are detrimental to the present by amending what "can be" righted and facing what cannot be. Personal responsibility allows a person to accept what they have done as bad decisions with bad consequences, rather than the only course of action available to a bad person. Commitment to this new freedom is instilled. "The light at the end of the tunnel" may not be a train after all.

PHASE 5
New Education

New education[†] would be information[†] that may have not been considered. At this point the program should have created the basis for exploration and growth. Basic life skills are addressed and refined. The future is planned with confidence in, instead of fear of, consequences.

Change is the essence[†] of this phase. New attitudes, behaviors, feelings and dreams have been explored. Goals are set and boundaries are developing. Accomplishments are real and measurable. Mornings begin a journey without fear and evenings are spent in gratitude rather than regret.

Dedication is the main goal of this phase. With it comes the required decision to strive to do life today without the fear and pain of yesterday. The resolution of issues gives a sense of freedom to approach each new day expecting it to be achievable. If the new information received is implemented[†], a new life will emerge. Practice using the new information received will result in refinement of the skills associated. Many people have never consciously considered this maintenance concept. Many people don't require change in their life.

PHASE 6
Sponsorship

By sponsorship[†] we mean the ability to guide or lead by example. In the process of moving forward in life, we have developed from what we were, to what we have become. The ability to share this information with another is the payback we owe to the universe for the opportunity we have received. Someone who is new to this concept of change needs functional role models who can explain these concepts in basic terms.

Continued growth is the goal of this program. It is hoped that the information presented has been absorbed and has become a desire to grow. Completing this phase ultimately qualifies the participant to guide another through it. Continued involvement and implementation[†] will enhance and strengthen their reserve to maintain these new ideas that have been presented.

1

INFORMATION

(CLARIFICATION)

KNOWLEDGE IS POWER (YOURS)

KNOWLEDGE: *a result or product of knowing; information or understanding acquired through experience; ability or skill; cognition.*

—The sum total of what you know.

IGNORANT: *lacking knowledge or comprehension of the thing specified; unaware; uninformed.*

—The deliberate denial of knowledge or, not knowing any better.

Life is constant assimilation[†] of information[†]. We vary greatly in what is of interest to us and how we process it. One thing sure, we all have the ability to learn. This process begins when we are children and first realize that there is something out there. Some of us are taught to wonder while others of us are taught not to ask. As we develop we store information in different ways. Some ask and understand while others have to experience things to remember them. Lies can have a devastating effect on how we process information, much the same as painful experiences do. If we lie to ourselves, for whatever reason, we begin to doubt our ability to understand or believe what is presented to us. This is especially true if what we see or hear substantiates[†] our fear of why we first lied to ourselves. Part of dependency is "denial." D. E. N. I. A. L. In recovery[†] it means, "Don't Even Notice I Am Lying." Knowledge of dependence will not stop a person from denying it, but it may allow them to begin to believe the facts regarding recovery.

The basis for what we know, really know, is knowledge. I

was in the train station at Lansing, Michigan in the late 60's talking to a ticket agent named J. Red Robinson. He said, "No man should walk the path of life in bondage for the lack of knowledge". Since that day his statement has stayed with me. Sometimes it has plagued me in its truth, for we cannot claim ignorance of what we already know. It's too bad ignorance is not more immediately painful. Perhaps we as a people would not lean so heavily on it as an excuse if the consequences were more rapidly apparent. I believe ignorance to be the deliberate denial of knowledge or the refusal to learn.

This program was developed through the search for meaning and understanding of dependent persons who are caught in the downward spiral of their disease.[†] If you have no use today for what is being presented, I urge you to attempt to at least understand the information as one day you may have a need for it. There are no dumb questions. If the answers are not available to you today, search for them. In today's world there are inexhaustible stores of information available to us. We are continually learning and recording if only in our own minds, vast amounts of fact and opinion. What are being presented to you here are facts as I believe them. The dilemma of dependence is of ongoing concern to me. New information is becoming available to those afflicted as well as those who treat the dependent. No one has all the answers. If you find something here that works for you, run with it. If not, save it. Someday it may be of importance to you or one you care for. It is certain that nothing presented here can hinder you on your journey through life. Good luck!

DISEASE CONCEPT OF
CHEMICAL DEPENDENCY

Elvin Morton Jellinek (1890-1963)

Elvin Morton Jellinek or most often, E. M. Jellinek, was a bio-statistician (study of the statistical probabilities of biological organisms) physiologist (a branch of biology that deals with the functions and activities of life or of living matter) and an alcoholism researcher. He was born in New York City and died at the desk of his study at Stanford University on 22 October, 1963.

He was fluent in nine languages and could communicate in four others. From 1941 to 1952, he was Associate Professor of Applied Physiology at Yale University. In 1952, he was engaged by the World Health Organization in Geneva as a consultant on alcoholism, and made significant contributions to the work of the alcoholism sub-committee of the W.H.O.'s Expert Committee on Mental Health. The World Health Organization (WHO) is a specialized agency of the United Nations (UN) that acts as a coordinating authority on international public health.

Upon his retirement from the W.H.O. in the late 1950's, he returned to the USA. In 1958, he joined the Psychiatry Schools of both the University of Toronto and the University of Alberta, and in 1962, he moved to Stanford University in California, where he remained until his death.

In 1946 Jellinek defined alcoholism (C/D) as "Any use that causes any damage to the individual or to society[†] or both." He was greatly responsible for alcoholism (C/D) being understood as a disease[†] and not a personal defect, and was one of the first to apply the medical model to dependence. In essence[†] he said, "Hey, world, you mislabeled this thing. You put it in the weakness category, and it really belongs on the disease list."

The way we label things has a large effect on how we see them, what we expect from them, and our actions regarding them. I like the analogy of beans. Whether a bean is labeled pinto or coffee will make a big difference. Depending on which I think it is will determine how I consume it. Very different results are expected from each. A mistake could lead to a disastrous tasting beverage or a stimulating bitter chip dip. Using the term disease[†] has some drawbacks to most people. We usually have sympathy for a person suffering from a disease and we don't usually think that someone has become ill willingly. We don't criticize people who are suffering the symptoms of a disease nor do we expect them to fulfill all the responsibilities that they normally have. It is generally accepted that sick people should be provided care for their illness and that being ill is not a pleasurable experience.

Medically in order for a condition to meet the criteria of a disease it must be;

1. Progressive: increasing in extent or severity

2. Symptomatic: having identifiable characteristic

3. Chronic[†]: weakening or habitual

4. Can be fatal if not treated

It must be understood that some of the actions of the C/D person are unwillful and symptomatic. This does not in any way lessen their responsibility for these actions and they must be held accountable for their decisions. Accepting this responsibility can become a major stuck point, or obstacle, when dealing with Chemical Dependency. Many C/D people find themselves being forced to pay the consequences of their behavior. Until the person is willing to accept their part in their problem, recovery is improbable.

Jellinek's work was updated in 1983 by George E. Vaillant in

"The Natural History of Alcoholism." This update represented the work begun by Jellinek more than 30 years earlier and is based on two groups of men. One group, called the college sample, was composed of Yale University students. The other group, called the core city sample, was composed of men from high-crime inner-city neighborhoods. Members of both groups developed alcoholism. This brought up the question, "What are the factors that distinguish those who develop C/D from those who don't?" Vaillant determined by the results of this study that those who developed C/D didn't necessarily come from impoverished backgrounds or necessarily have any pre-existing personality or psychological problems. As for the predictors of C/D, the most significant determinants were found to be a family history of dependence or having been raised in a culture with a high rate of C/D.

To further reinforce and explain the medical model of Chemical Dependency the Judges & Lawyers Assistance Program (JLAP) of Indianapolis, Indiana has listed the characteristics of any dependency as:

> **1.** Primary Disease: The disease itself causes drinking or drug use. It is not secondary to some other disease or mental illness.

> **2.** Chronic[†]: There is no cure for the disease, but it can be treated and controlled. It demands a change in behavior.

> **3.** Progressive: The disease always gets worse, it does not get better, and there is no turning back and beginning all over again as if one never drank or used.

> **4.** Fatal: This is a fatal disease if not controlled. It always leads to premature death and serious health problems even if death certificate indicates the cause of death to be one of the complications of the disease, e.g., heart problems, liver failure, bleeding ulcers, etc.

5. Treatable: The disease can be controlled if the drinking or drug use stops. It is much like diabetes in the sense that if the body chemistry is stabilized by not drinking or using, the dependent person may lead a normal life.

6. Relapse is Common.

7. Genetics Play a Part: Since 1980, many studies corroborate genetic or familial predisposition to the disease.

8. Denial is a hallmark of the disease.

This modern vernacular† explains more of the symptoms required to meet the disease criteria or qualification. I personally question the lack of explanation for Characteristic #6: Relapse is Common. As in any life threatening disease, relapse is only common if proper medical procedures and recovery or rehabilitation techniques are not followed. It may be better said that if ignored, relapse is common.

A change occurs when an otherwise healthy organism develops a disease; therefore, it would follow that a change must likewise occur to restore it to health. Participating in, or at least being aware of, this change would greatly improve one's chance of not relapsing.

TYPES OF
CHEMICAL DEPENDENCY

a.k.a. Jellinek's Species

ALPHA(Problem Drinking Or Using): Purely psychological dependence. Neither loss of control or inability to abstain. Use is relied upon to deal with life's problems. Possible problems with work, school, family, friends and relationships. Progression is not inevitable†.

BETA: Not physically or psychologically dependent but physical problems are evident. Cirrhosis, gastritis, tracks, deviated septum, speed bumps, etc. Heavy use and inadequate diet are primary causes.

GAMMA: Marked by change in tolerance, withdrawal symptoms and loss of control. Progression from psychological to physical dependence. Most detrimental physically and socially. The Jellinek curve is representative of this phase of dependency. Most prominent type in USA. Most common in 12 Step Recovery Programs.

DELTA: Like GAMMA without loss of control, rather an inability to abstain. Amount of consumption may be predicted at any given time. Withdrawal symptoms inevitable at cessation.

EPSILON: Binge Drinking Or Using = Periodic Dependence.

---

* ALPHA and EPSILON may be symptoms of other psychological disorders in and of themselves and do not necessarily determine dependency.

*GAMMA and DELTA have features indicative of a disease.

E.Jellinek

PHASES OF
CHEMICAL DEPENDENCY

by E.M. Jellinek

PRE-DEPENDENCE PHASE

Use is socially motivated. Person will look for situations where use is accepted or will probably occur. Use becomes the common way to deal with stress. Behavior appears normal to outside observers. This phase can extend from several months to many years. An increase in tolerance gradually occurs.

Social use
Occasional relief use
Heavy habitual social (or occupational) use
Constant relief use commences
Increase in tolerance
First blackout

PRODROMAL PHASE (Warning or signal)

Sneaking starts. Begin use before a party or to set your mood or mask amount of use. Use becomes heavy without being necessarily obvious. Effort is required to "LOOK" right to observers. This phase can last from 6 months to 4 or 5 years depending on circumstances.

Dependence increases
Secret use increases
Repeated D.U.I.
Urgency to use
Guilt or shame about use
Unable to discuss use (Denial)
Blackouts increase
Loss of control (Decrease of ability to stop when others do)

CRUCIAL or BASIC PHASE

Using begins a chain reaction. User usually cannot control the amount of use once he or she begins. They still can control whether or not they will use. Use is obviously different to the observer so excuses and rationalizations are necessary. Efforts to regain control begin: i.e., deliberate abstinence, geographical changes, and job or school changes. As a rule, nothing works for an extended period of time and user will return to previous patterns of use or worse. The user's general response to these failures is remorse, resentment and aggression. First hospitalization or institutionalization usually occurs during this phase.

Use explained with excuses
Grandiose and aggressive behavior
Constant remorse
Efforts to control use fail repeatedly
Promises and resolutions fail
Tries geographical escapes
Loss of other interests
Family and friends avoided
Work (or school) troubles
Money problems associated with use
Unreasonable resentments
Neglect of food
Loss of self-esteem
Loss of ordinary will-power
Morning use (need, not choice)
Decrease in tolerance
Physical deterioration

CHRONIC PHASE

Final phase of dependency (and possibly life). Use will become constant and continual. Social status collapses. Life is lived on the fringes of society†. Tolerance is sporadic at best.

Simple tasks are impossible without use. Paranoia reins. User's rationalization system fails. Use continues because user cannot imagine any way out of their dilemma.

Continuous use
Moral deterioration
Impaired thinking
Unreasonable fears (paranoia)
Use with outcasts
Physical and mental damage
Inability to initiate action
Obsession with use
Vague spiritual desires
All alibis exhausted
Complete defeat admitted

INEVITABLE DEATH!

Jellinek and others, including this author, emphasize that persons do not have to reach any particular stage of dependence in order to successfully recover and develop a meaningful and productive manner of living! C/D has been proven to be a progressive, terminal disease if left untreated. Medical science may someday find a cure but it has not yet!

JELLINEK'S CURVE

PRE-DEPENDENCE PHASE

──────────────── GREAT RISK ────────────────
PRODROMAL PHASE
(WARNING)

──────────────── RATIONAL RISK ────────────────
CRUCIAL PHASE
(BASIC)

──────────────── LOW RISK ────────────────
CHRONIC PHASE

LAST CHANCE

The top of the graph would seem to indicate a greater risk upon entering a recovery lifestyle than the bottom. I believe this to be factual in that; in the early stages of dependency, our lives are still reasonably functional. It involves a greater risk to abandon what, so far, has worked for us. Recovery involves changing your playgrounds, playmates and playthings. If a person's current lifestyle is still acceptably functional, how can they be expected to abandon it for an unknown new reality? Herein lays the risk factor. In the later phases of harmful dependency, there's nothing left to lose and everything to gain. The opposite is true in the early phases "Potentially" there is everything to lose, and nothing to gain! The reality of recovery is, "It's never too early, nor is it ever too late!" (UNLESS YOU DIE!)

PHASES OF RECOVERY

Jellinek and Vaillant did a great service to the recovery community in their studies but one of the major concerns of C/D education† and treatment was beyond their scope of knowledge. I refer to the "Recovery Curve." The Jellinek report and subsequent studies deal in great depth with C/D clients regarding the extent of their involvement in dependency. Without addressing the correlation to a particular place or commitment to recovery they inspire new questions.

I have been asked many times to explain the relevance of the curve or "V" shape of most graphs depicting Jellinek's work. The downward slide, both moral and spiritual of the dependent person is well defined and documented. The questions I have encountered most often are regarding the other side of the curve or "V." I choose to call this region the "Recovery Curve." There appear to be four main phases of rebuilding a life ravaged by Chemical Dependency. They are 1) Admission†, 2) Inventory†, 3) Recovery†, 4) Acceptance of a new way of life. They are not placed on the graph herein because they are not relative to the stage of dependency you enter recovery. The most important fact to know is that the earlier or sooner you enter recovery, the less damage you will have done. It's NEVER too late - and it's never TOO early.

1

ADMISSION of a problem, powerlessness, or defeat, is primary to future phases. If we cannot, or will not, acknowledge that a problem exists, there is no problem. It's really that simple. Every C/D person has stood on the premise that chemicals are not the problem, they are the solution. When a particular chemical negatively affects our lives to the point that rationalization and even denial fails to work, we find a new chemical or behavior to achieve the familiar result. That is; not feeling our true feelings or accepting our proper station in life. ERGO: If we accept no responsibility, how can we expect to be trusted to act responsibly? The dependent person not only expects it, they demand it! They believe that they have a choice. The only choice they really have is when to use again. They cannot be sure within themselves when this will happen, only that it will. Lack of confidence, coupled with questionable self-esteem, has destroyed many good intentions. To admit defeat is not a pleasurable feeling. The fear of the unknown can be overwhelming. The early stages of C/D (Pre-dependent stage) involve a great risk in this admission. Life is not yet out of control, the drugs and behaviors still work. Why then take such a great risk in committing to this recovery thing? Life's not really broken yet, why fix it? This perhaps is the greatest obstacle to helping our pre-dependent youth. I believe the risk can be substantially reduced by proper and meaningful education[†]. The "Just Say No" approach has not worked, nor has it restored our faith in the Easter Bunny. It stood the same chance of doing either. Young people are not the naive children we would like to believe. They have already taken their first steps into adulthood. Our job is to inform them of their direction. They must take the initiative to change. They will not be steered. This is their life, they make the decisions. If presented properly and honestly, we can inform them of their options as well as consequences. To try to force this admission from them is like setting a child in the corner, all they learn is what we want from them. As a child I had to burn my fingers to learn what hot meant. As an adult I still need to be burned occasionally, or live a non-eventful life. The lesson is that hot is hot. Just becoming an adult, tough, smart, rich or powerful does not make hot any less hot. No one gets to control the temperature of the flame. The control is in where you put your fingers and how long you keep them there! Knowledge, not manipulation[†] is where success lies. The admission that the flame is hot is an admission of powerlessness only if we repeatedly are burning our hands. The social partier has little if any trouble not using if they have a reason. Even the party animal can stop given a strong enough reason. The dependent person, however, is the one continually burning their hand, the ones who cannot accept life for what it is. Their salvation is in the escape they have found in chemicals or repugnant† behaviors. During the time that these behaviors are functioning for them, it is extremely difficult to facilitate change. The less personally acceptable these behaviors are, the greater the chance of change. This is better accomplished by education† than forced compliance. Either way, the consequences of behaviors must be assigned to the person taking the action. Immediate families or society† as a whole cannot accept responsibility for the perpetrator. This action will only re-affirm freedom from responsibility to the dependent person. Powerlessness is hard to accept when little or no power is felt in one's life. Some people can only claim the power to fail or chose to do wrong. There is a tendency to hold on desperately to the power to break rules, if that is the only power felt. To educate people to the fact that admitting powerlessness, is in fact empowering, gives them the opportunity to make decisions and commitments based on the hope of a better more fulfilling life. The farther down the Jellinek Curve people have gone, the more receptive they become to taking the risk of admitting their problem and considering recovery. Education is the only tool society has that can circumvent the dependent's slide.

2

PERSONAL INVENTORY† is critical in recovery from any dependency. Without this type of inventory the dependent person has no knowledge of what they have to work with. One of the greatest problems of the dependent is the depth of the denial they have existed in. After a long enough experience, reality can become so blurred that the insanity is more believable than the truth. By taking a thorough enough inventory the dependent begins to separate fact from fiction. Without a guide, able counselor, or another who has been down this particular road, the dependent is sure to become lost in the wasteland of denial. The best attempt at self-honesty cannot hope to approach the self-deception that the dependent is used to. The phrase, "Cunning, Baffling and Powerful" is perhaps the best current definition of Chemical Dependency. To lie when the truth is more convenient is the motto of many dependent people. If enough lies are told, reality becomes lost in the fog of deception. Reality actually becomes the perpetuation of the deception. This is the critical juncture for the counselor. How do we confront the deception of the dependent without destroying their reality as they have come to believe? This procedure is less difficult if we have ourselves traveled this road. It must be understood that no one has ever taken an honest thorough inventory for another. The motivation must exist in the dependent or an impasse has been reached. We can lead by example, support with our own strengths and educate from our knowledge, but the unwilling will not be moved. To exert too much force is to rob the dependent of their experience and minimize its importance. Once learned, this ability to take an honest self-inventory becomes an asset to life. If occurring as a result of manipulation[†] or outside pressure, the inventory becomes our agenda, not the dependents!

3

RECOVERY is now an option. The dependent at this point knows "who" they are. This knowledge is empowering and well deserved. An honest inventory[†] has smashed many long standing beliefs and reaffirmed many more. Most importantly it has identified to the inventory taker the nature of their personality. This knowledge opens many doors. Although the dependent has achieved the right to make reality based decisions, they are not forced to make them. Many people, at this point, settle for "good enough" mental health or recovery. For a myriad[†] of reasons a stall point may be reached. The greatest of these reasons is fear. Now that the dependent has dismantled their life and looked at all the pieces, they feel they have achieved a level of understanding that will keep them from repeating the same patterns of behavior and thinking that got them into trouble or discomfort. This may be true for some, but for the dependent, subtracting from their repertoire[†] of tricks without replacing them with functional new behaviors is a recipe for relapse. To restructure a belief system is no small task. The dependent's greatest fear is that having done this restructuring, life as they know it, still will not work. What if all the beliefs that have been working for them are based on dysfunctional information? This must be considered! It is at this point that the most serious and desperate blaming may occur. It may be the counselors fault for bringing the dependent to this point, or the parents fault for not properly preparing the dependent for life. It is important to note that at this point, when no one is accusatory, that the dependent may reach so deep into their defenses as to accuse another of causing their dilemma. The dilemma is that recovery can be a terrifying option. Recovery is a restructuring of one's-self. It is using the information[†] gleaned[†] from the inventory process to enhance one's knowledge of life. In the knowledge is the power to re-create. It also includes the wisdom to know your shortcomings and the strength to ask for assistance. It is the ability to decide what you are to be. Recovery can sometimes be the first good habit some people get. It's fearful and rewarding. Seen through, it reaffirms who you are and allows you the choice of what you are to become.

4

ACCEPTANCE of a new way of life is the final phase of recovery. Webster defines acceptance as: "the quality or state of being accepted," or "to receive willingly." Utilizing the new knowledge of themselves, the dependent has achieved a level of understanding and responsibility that allows them a new freedom of choice. They have at least begun to establish healthy boundaries that can guide their actions and confirm their beliefs. What they are, or are to become, is finally acceptable in the eyes of their peers as well as society[†]. This final phase of recovery is not an end, but rather a beginning, of a new way of life. Acceptance does not necessarily mean longevity or competency. This new found lifestyle requires practice. No one is able to perform perfectly at all times. There will be failures. These are the times when the dependent's commitments will be tried. It is at these times that a support group of peers is invaluable. Dependents that have faced these uncertainties and overcome them are usually willing to be of assistance to others. In 12 Step programs this is referred to as sharing[†] your experience strength and hope. In order to be of service to others, you as a dependent must first have had the experience of taking these actions. In resolving our life experiences in recovery we become able leaders only if our own lives are in order. The inventory phase is basic in achieving and maintaining this balance.

IMPLEMENTATION

(DISCOVERY)

RESPECT

RESPECT: *an act of giving particular attention; Consideration: high or special regard; Esteem: the quality or state of being esteemed; worthy or valued.*

—To allow another their belief or feelings without interference. To accept my level or place in another person's world. Admiration, awe, or empathy of another person's position in life.

"I don't get any respect around here!" How many times have you felt this way? Have you ever said it? This phrase is most often used when a person doesn't feel that they are being heard or acknowledged about something. It's used often when directives or orders are not being followed.

To respect something is to acknowledge or pay some amount of attention to it. Respect cannot be an accident, it must be directed. This acknowledgement or attention is responsive toward a person, place or thing. Respect is felt about, shown for, directed toward, or paid to a thing because it is due or deserves it, not because it is demanded. Forced compliance is intimidation, not respect. Many famous philosophers have theorized at length about respect. Usually I get brain freeze trying to understand, and put into normal life, their concepts. To expound without explanation is baffling and condescending to me.

Respect usually has something to do with a behavior. In respecting an object, we often give it a certain amount of influence or control over us. This influences our thoughts and feelings to behave in an appropriate manor. This behavior could include refraining from certain treatment of the object or acting only in particular ways in connection with it; ways that are regarded as fitting, deserved by, or owed to the object. There are many ways to respect things: keeping our distance from them; helping them, praising or emulating them; obeying or abiding by them; not violating or interfering with them; protecting or being careful with them, talking about them in ways that reflect worth or status; mourning them; nurturing[†] them. Acting in respectful ways without respecting the object or other person is manipulation[†] and not honest.

Respect can be broken into three categories, "by", "of" and "for". Respect "by" can be envy or fear. Respect "of" is much broader and includes authority, society[†], and self. Respect "for" can stand alone or be combined with one of the other types. The primary or basic difference in these three types of respect is reason.

Respect "by" doesn't take much thought or reason. It is usually demanded and to a degree, automatic or reactive. Awe or intimidation are two examples. These can be products of an individual's own low self-worth or lack of esteem. They can be real or imagined. These are types of respect that have no real worth, but are, in fact, very real. The common thread in "by" respect is power. It is more a means of control than a bestowed honor. "I can hurt you," "I'm famous," "I'm in charge" or "I'll ruin you" are a few examples of "by" respect. Some people don't understand this type of respect. Lack of, or low self-respect makes people unnecessarily susceptible to this type of oppression. This type of person often finds himself or herself questioning their place in life. Some resign themselves to this state; others resent it, but remain unchanged. They never understand that what they know as respect is incomplete. They have never seen or been taught the whole meaning of the concept of respect.

Respect "of" is felt or inspired and is based on values. There is a basis in fact for it. It is not necessarily deserved by appointment or circumstance. It cannot be demanded or required. It can be necessary, but it must be honestly given. Nearly all children have someone they respect. This is "of" respect, until they reach the age of reason when they begin to understand their part and place in life. Unfortunately, many people have no real concept of this type of respect, either because they have never seen it practiced, or they have never been taught about it. If a person cannot understand this type of respect, they cannot earn it from other people. It is a value.

Respect "for" is a logical consideration of a person, place or thing. It is not based on feelings. "We" have respect "for" things because they have shown reason to be respected. This type of respect can be independent of our person in that we may respect someone due to their accomplishments without any knowledge of their motivation. As an artist or musician that we hear or see, and appreciate, without any knowledge of their personal motivations or values.

Authority does not automatically include respect. Authority without responsibility is not respectable, it's reproachable. Compliance may be mandatory[†], respect cannot be governed. All that respect of authority means is willful compliance. If something is against your will, the question you must ask yourself is "What is best for all concerned?" If no one were in a position of authority, chaos would rule. Only the strong would survive, and not for long. We all need each other in one way or another. Everyone is led by someone. A wise person knows whom they are following.

Society[†] does not automatically deserve respect, nor do all its laws. In order to survive, laws must be enforced. If all our laws were fair, we would live in an ideal society. Unfortunately, our constant changing of the rules is not always in the best interest of all peoples. You can, however, rest assured that the changes are in the interest of those who make them. "Personal gain" and "prestige" were buzzwords of the 80's. Perhaps this current generation will begin the transformation of our society into one of wholeness and common good. What is life without a dream?

Self-respect is never constant. It incorporates all aspects of our lives. The people we know and associate with, the things we do, say, feel and believe, even the way we communicate. Self-respect is honesty. It's like a mirror. If we respect, for good reason, what we see in the mirror, we have self-respect. Self-respect is all encompassing. It is as small as our most insignificant parts and as large as our greatest abilities. It's not based on what you have so much as on how you use it. If we have self-respect we "own" our statements and behaviors even when they are incorrect. They are part of the image in the mirror we see.

Under the heading of self-respect is responsive respect. If you, as a person, do not agree with a statement, you have the option not to respond. If a person in authority has made this statement, and expects a response, you may be insubordinate in not responding. Is responsive respect required? Is it polite? Is it expected? These are only hypothetical questions without more information. The underlying question is, "Considering the subject and the players, do I need or want to participate?" Do I feel strongly enough about my convictions to take an adversarial stand? Am I required by law or duty to respond? At times responsive respect becomes a trap. We usually set it for ourselves and step in it when confronted by a situation we have participated in. Common situations might be, "Why are you late?" or "Where have you been?" Your response, or lack thereof, says a lot about you and what kind of person you feel like at the time. Ideally these are learning experiences and not often repeated. Self-esteem keeps us from re-acting these types of behaviors (hopefully).

In an ideal society respect is a basic rule. In our society† we have tried to make it law. The only people who have profited by this have been the lawmakers, who are often viewed with contempt until we need their help. Respect has earned a price tag in America. Our system of values has dropped so far as to allow criminals to become heroes, and real courage to be viewed as foolish. The old adage, "I got no dog in that fight" shows no respect for others as well as an absence of self-respect. If the fight is in your neighborhood, you got a dog in it! Does this mean that any one person deserves respect all the time? "I don't think so!!!!" You as a person are worthy of as much respect as you have for others. This is a basic fact.

TYPES OF RESPECT: EXAMPLE:

by _____   _____

of _____   _____

for _____   _____

self _____   _____

authoritarian_____   _____

societal _____   _____

SPIRITUALITY

SPIRITUALITY: the quality or state of being spiritual.

—The absence of self-centeredness, an inner drive towards wholeness and harmony.

SPIRITUAL: of, relating to, consisting of, or affecting the spirit.

—Your core self.

SPIRIT: the immaterial intelligent (mental) or sentient (aware) part of a person.

—Your soul or Ch'i.

RELIGION: the service and worship of God, or the supernatural, in an organized manner.

—Organized spirituality.

Spirituality[†] is not a religious concept, but organized religion[†] "is" a spiritual concept. In my life spirituality has proven to be more of an asset than a burden. This is not meant to imply that I have reached any great level or pinnacle of spirituality, but rather that it has become a comfortable part of my daily existence. To have found a balance of spirituality and self-caring has enriched my life beyond my greatest expectations. Upon entering recovery, I had little, if any, of either! To understand this concept enables me to allow for the possibility that what I believe could be in error. This would mean, of course, that there "may be" another concept of life that I have no knowledge of at this time. This awareness along with a minor degree of willingness[†] was the beginning of my spirituality.

I believe the basis of spirituality to be giving. By this I do not mean bargaining, but rather giving freely without expecting repayment. It would be doing what I know to be intrinsically[†] right when being less honorable would be easier. It is foregoing gain, for a sense of harmony. Spirituality is not always easy, but it's always right. It is not to be contended or measured by mere mortals with their self-serving agendas. You cannot define it without minimizing its potential. I do not believe you can exist without it, although we have the capacity to ignore its presence. This universal awareness has been instilled in every human creature at birth yet often it seems to be better preserved and practiced in the wild. Animals do not appear to be as polluted as humans when it comes to spirituality. They "are," and that seems to be enough for them. Perhaps we as intelligent creatures have lost the concept of spirituality, or perhaps it has become less convenient to us in our endless pursuit of money, power and prestige.

From a religious or ecclesiastical[†] perspective[†], spirituality would mean a closeness or oneness with a Supreme Being. This being may take many forms, but there appears to be a common thread in all religions that says, "This Higher Power, if you will, is the be all and end all of everything and anything". This Power is either everything or it is nothing. Although I personally agree with this assumption I in no way demand that you, the reader, or anyone else must assume my stance or belief.

It has been said, "If there were no God, mankind would invent one". This concept lends credence[†] to the fact that spiritual dilemmas are not always solved rationally or justly. Those who choose to participate in an organized religion[†] are urged to be spiritually aware at all times. To some this is the ticket to heaven or eternal bliss of some sort. To others it is the only way of redemption from their past transgressions. One belief is that those who do not conform will be banished to a bad place to suffer for what they have, or have not done. To me the intent of these religious rules is to promote spirituality. Not a bad concept by any means and entirely necessary for some. If a Higher Power made an error in creating us, it may have been endowing us with free will. It could be said that religion is the fear of God; spirituality is the love of God.

A popular song of the 60's said, "You make your own heaven or hell right here on earth." This statement may be more factual than some care to admit. I have seen life from the depths of depravity, where nothing mattered and no one cared. Still somehow a spark of spirituality glowed. Somehow I knew within myself that something was amiss. Usually it was my self-will run riot that had caused my pain. I had failed to consider the spiritual force within myself and had based my decisions on self-centered concerns. I did this often and willfully for many years. There was seldom any worthwhile pay-off. Life continually got darker and more painful. The dreams I had were worthless ones, my mansions built on sand. I got my spirituality by default, not from virtue.

I was raised in a Christian family. For this I will always be grateful. The Christian education† I received had little, if any effect on my actions as a teenager or afterwards. Why not? What started out a part time thing consumed my every thought. Living a life of excess became a habit, as did mood-altering chemicals. I took a wild ride on the dysfunction-go-round of life without a ticket to get off. It took me years to figure out that the ride was out of control, the switch had jammed full tilt. It seemed natural, because I had been there for so long, to keep hanging on. The dream had become a nightmare and I would not wake up. It felt macho to continue the ride when everyone else with even a dim vision of reality had long ago jumped off. This was not a lonely ride at the beginning. The loneliness I felt at the end was overwhelming!

Spirituality has become the basis for recovery as I know it. It may not be a requirement for yours. It has simplified my reasons for living and helped me establish functional boundaries. It has allowed me to accept and forgive the frailties of others as well as my own. It has directed me towards a peace where-in true serenity abides. This peace that passes understanding is not always at my beck and call. Often it seems life can be unfair, sometimes it is downright cruel. One thing I am sure of, whatever life has in store for me today cannot be made any better if I use mood-altering drugs to escape reality. A few moments of silent meditation can begin to re-balance my state of reality. This is not a cure or an escape, but rather work that must be done to maintain a sense of wholeness. The less trying times of life can only be more rewarding if I keep my ego, as well as my temper in check. Meditation takes me out of self and into wholeness. No one is perfect. I do not think perfection would be very interesting. I just try to live one day at a time to the best of my ability. This seems to give me a sense of gratitude each night when I lie down to sleep. Spirituality has removed fear and shame from my life by giving me means to resolve those issues that cause them. Just having the means does not do anything. I must be honest, open and willing to use them.

The world is full of kings and queens, who'll blind your eyes and steal your dreams. When I abandoned Christianity, I turned my back on spirituality as I understood it. Even though I was not consciously aware of it, spirituality was always there influencing my life. Today it is a powerful, conscious part of my existence. It has given me an inner freedom from the chains that bound me to the past and allowed me to move forward to a more serene state of being. Spirituality is all that's good and right about life. Spirituality is all about serenity: that peace within that seems to multiply when it is freely offered to others. It is not about earning recognition, power or wealth, it's not about keeping score, or accomplishing anything. Spirituality is about being O.K. with whom you are and where you're going. Where you have been doesn't really matter in a spiritual sense. Religion† is for those who are afraid of going to hell. To me, raw spirituality is for those who have already been there.

CONSEQUENCES

CONSEQUENCES: a conclusion derived from logic, something that is necessarily following from a set of conditions.

—The natural course of events ("For every action, there is an opposite and equal re-action" - Newton's Third Law of Motion).

Understanding consequences is an insight based in history. They can be a just reward or a dirty word depending on the perspective[†] of the beliefs and historical events that surround them. Consequences must be accepted in life. They are relevant[†] to any action we take or thought we have. As a tool for learning, consequences are invaluable. Whether a blessing or curse, they remain a real and important part of anyone's life.

History determines one's understanding of, and belief in, consequences. If a concept of consequence is developed in youth, great benefits may be realized in adulthood. Failure to instill this concept in youth may be a primary cause of many prevalent dysfunctions our society[†] has to deal with today regarding its young citizens. As children develop, consequences create boundaries to deter improper conduct. Without knowledge of, and practical application of, this tool, children may become adults without social skills required to fit into society. This is the foundation of many splinter factions that we see in today's society. The adage, "Misery loves company," speaks for itself. To be most effective, consequences must be consistent without inflexibility. They must be rational and understandable. Much insight into human action can be gleaned[†] from the understanding of consequences.

Accepting responsibility for one's consequences without rationalization or minimization is a focal point in mental health. It falls under the category of being, or becoming, accountable. In some instances, a person can only handle the accountability of one day. In some instances, one day can have life altering consequences. Every day we pass many crossroads. The paths we choose determine the consequences we must face. Consequences are not necessarily punishments; they are the logical result of a behavior.

Consequences are a direct result of one's choices in action and thought, they seldom, if ever, are random. If the weather outside is rainy and you have to be in it, the consequence of getting wet is not always a necessity. If you prepare for the weather, you can be less affected by it. In this manner, our consequences are rational, predictable and understandable. From a logical perspective[†], consequences teach us to deal with situations from a historical viewpoint. Negative consequences to an action "should" result in different courses of future action. This is, of course, logical, not necessarily practical. If a person has no knowledge of positive re-enforcement, that person may indeed repeat negatively rewarded behavior for its familial value. That being, "It's what's always been, how can it be anything else?" The possibility of "something else" is a key to change and self-empowerment. Understanding of that reality, and practice in its regard, are imperative to change.

Consequences can be one of life's jackpots or one of its catastrophes. It is all a matter of perspective. If care is taken to be in safe places doing honorable things, the chances of negative consequences are minimized. This concept can be a turning point in any life, particularly the life of one confronted with dependency. The equation of consequence to a dependent person is short-circuited to, "I need something. How shall I obtain it?" The consequence of that thought process, or the actions required to achieve the desired result, is of no matter until the consequences become unbearable. Only at that time does an effected person consider consequence. "I promise I'll never do it again," echoes through our society[†] as addicts and alcoholics beg for one more chance with less consequence. Education[†] is the only real alternative.

Our overpopulated prisons are full of prisoners who have been told that the consequence of their behavior is incarceration. In reality, incarceration is their punishment. Their consequences are not so evident. Knowledge of the true concept of consequences is all but lost in today's society. This information[†] properly utilized could have a profound[†] impact on not only our prison populations, but also in our rates of recidivism. Accepting the theory of consequential inevitability could empower and encourage meaningful change in any person. Understanding and implementation[†] of this theory by our criminal courts could begin a new, relevant[†] and more functional system that we may proudly, once again, call our Justice System. Right behavior with the understanding and expectation of positive consequences will do more to heal our society than any amount of punishment.

Consequences have always been and will always be. Better understanding of one's history and behavioral patterns will lead them to a more predictable set of circumstances. It is hoped that personal accountability will create an atmosphere of dependability, whereby one may enjoy true freedom and peace wherever they may be.

Ignoring or extolling[†] consequence is folly, for tomorrow holds a new set of circumstances and a new series of consequences.

BALANCE (HOMEOSTASIS)

HOMEOSTASIS: *a relatively stable state of equilibrium or a tendency toward such a state.*

BALANCE: *stability produced by even distribution of weight on each side of a vertical axis.*

—How well you roll with the punches.

Balance is precarious[†] to say the least. Even Wallenda slipped. It cost him his life. Our lives are at times at risk when we are not in balance. Life without a center point is out of control. Human beings need a point of reference, a center-point to return to, and a place where there is understanding if not peace. Many people have no point in their lives where these things were available. Many others have discarded the values or understanding of this point due to trauma or stress. Some are hospitalized, some are miserable and some are dead. What happened matters less than how a person copes with today.

Life at its very best, is balance. Balance is necessary for function. Function is relative to experience. If a person has no experience with balance, they find a way to exist without it. This could describe a myriad[†] of mental illnesses, unfortunate circumstances and insecurities. Life without balance is like flying a rock. No amount of energy will make you successful. Rock flying will never achieve balance. A rock's balance is on the ground, not in the air. People achieve balance in reality not in fantasy. If you cannot force a rock to fly, how can you force a human to balance?

Incarceration and hospitalization are both methods of forced compliance. It is a belief that hospitals are for healing and jails are for punishing. Based on that assumption, forced compliance does not work. Compliance must be willful and balance must be earned. To earn balance a person must learn what it is, or was, and strive to achieve it. To willfully live without seeking balance is the ultimate cowardice. Physical balance is required to maintain our physical health. Emotional balance is thereby required to maintain our emotional health. Emotional balance is needed to survive life's onslaught of stressful situations. Without healthy coping skills we lack function which may cause us to feel insecure and powerless. At these times of imbalance we are not in compliance with some universal law. We may eat too much or not enough. We may be victims or victimizers. These are the times in life when everything seems to be uphill. If you have ever felt this way, remember the moment and know that, if only for that very instant, you were a success, you knew one of the secrets of the universe. You were right, at that moment, it was, all uphill.

ATTITUDE

ATTITUDE: *a mental position with regard to a fact or state; a feeling or emotion with regard to a fact or state, i.e. your view of life in general or a particular situation, based on knowledge; a negative or hostile state of mind; a cocky or arrogant manner.*

—*Your response to outside stimuli or inside urge.*

I believe attitude to be a "present time" emotion. That is to say it is changeable at a moment's notice and dependent on outside stimuli as based in our own feelings. A peaceful safe attitude can instantly become one of fear and instability if confronted by violence. Happy-go-lucky people can become rude or angry in a moment when they feel confronted by a painful or fearful situation. Attitude is like an inner mirror. If we are content with our environment or circumstance, we emote† a reasonably mellow attitude. If we are surrounded by strife or uncertainty, our attitudes are probably less laid back. A sympathetic attitude can become instantly callous when we feel threatened.

Let's consider for a moment that a good attitude is one that mirrors a contented inner-self. A bad attitude then would imply threatening or unstable conditions. If we are happy, we generally have a reasonably pleasant attitude. It's usually when "something" is wrong that our attitudes turn ugly. A good barometer for our attitudes might be the degree of safety we feel. If we feel insecure, our attitudes can become defense mechanisms to protect our fragile feelings of self. I am not referring here to those situations where an aggressive situation develops into a need for self-protection. The dynamic I refer to is when our insecurities are stepped on inadvertently without knowledge of their sensitivity. We are responsible for our own feelings, and how we process them. How we allow others to affect them is up to us. If we carry around unresolved issues that leave us vulnerable to this type of unintentional attack, it's our responsibility to "not" react with unacceptable attitudes. Ideally we would be able to step back and respond, rather than react with a negative attitude. This is not an easy task, nor is it possible, until we understand what our issues are. This journey to wholeness starts with the first awareness. The first time we acknowledge that our attitude is not appropriate for the situation; we become empowered to make conscious decisions to change what inspired this type of action (attitude). The more we search inside ourselves for the motivations that move us, the more we become able to change them.

In the final analysis, we are in charge of our attitudes. We have the right, if not the power, to alter them to be more social. We also have the power to develop them to be more defensive if we have become a victim of others. They are ours. They are not our masters! We must take responsibility for our attitude and shape it to protect ourselves without being attacking or insulting to others.

CONFIDENCE

CONFIDENCE: *faith or belief that one will act in a right, proper or effective way, a quality or state of being certain; Syn: Assurance, Self-Possession, Aplomb† mean a state of mind or manner marked by easy coolness and freedom from uncertainty, diffidence† or embarrassment; confidence stresses faith in one's powers without any suggestion of conceit or arrogance.*

—Factually based belief, not an assumption.

Webster sure said a mouthful on this one. I am confident that he covered the topic in its entirety. He stated quite well what confidence is, however, he failed to explain "at all" where it comes from, how it is developed and when or how it varies.

Confidence without proof is the epitome† of ego. Confidence is based in action, either yours or others, and developed historically by word or deed. It is variable due to emotional and or physical change, situational by degrees.

I have confidence that the sun will rise. This is historical and I have personally experienced this action many times. The sunrise is variable due to weather and seasons. Some sunrises will be bright and warming; while at other times it may be obscured by clouds and rain. This analogy may seem simplistic, however if the sun didn't rise tomorrow, I would have less confidence of its appearance the next day.

People tend to lean toward confidence for security. If it always was, it will always be. From a recovery basis, no belief can be stronger or further from the truth. Although we have no control over the sunrise, we do have control over certain aspects of our lives. The fact that the sun has risen for millions of years gives one a sense that it will rise at least for the foreseeable future. There is real strength in that confidence. You can count on it to happen much the same as a person who uses mind altering chemicals for an extended period and, in fact, becomes dependent on that use, has confidence that they will remain dependent. A person lost in the desert has similar confidence that, although they rue the fact, the sun will rise and they will suffer.

"I can quit tomorrow" is runaway ego and denial if you are dependent on the use of mind altering chemicals. If you have real confidence, founded in fact and history, why not quit now? The fact is, one thing a dependent person has real confidence in, is that they cannot stop permanently. This person may have confidence that recovery is possible. They may believe that others may recover without having any confidence that they will personally be able to. The only way to achieve personal confidence is with proactive† action. A dedication to utilize the process of recovery that has worked with their peers is confidence in action.

As the sun will rise tomorrow, so shall you. New circumstance will emerge and new options will present themselves. Confidence is born in the successful completion of a single day, or even an hour. The true reward of confidence is accomplishment. As we build on this new personal confidence we begin to understand what has deterred us in the past from meaningful change. This change is not only a requirement but also a blessing. Real confidence will develop in us the ability to say no, or yes, as the case may be. We will look at situations with new knowledge and power when we feel confident. If we are building a life based on truth and harmony, we will achieve more than we could have dreamed before acquiring this knowledge. We now can feel the power of change. It no longer must be imagined, it is becoming part of our new being. As we practice these new skills from the most insignificant situations to the direst of circumstances their worth becomes invaluable. We will achieve what is required. We will succeed in this thing called life. We are capable; we will experience whatever life presents. We have confidence that the world will not only keep spinning, but that it is unfolding in our life to the exact degree that we participate.

Other's confidence of you is based on your history. Their trust in you is calculated as it relates to them. In order to increase the confidence that we instill in others, we must often create a new and more functional history in their eyes. It must be sufficient and of long enough duration to outweigh that which they have come to expect from us. Only in accomplishing this are we entitled to expect different responses from them. Words alone are not enough, we must act accordingly and with enough sincerity and longevity that they come to trust in what they see as a real change in our person. Confidence from others is seen as accomplishments, not works in progress.

Self-confidence proceeds confidence from others. Self confidence develops gradually as we become aware of this concept and implement[†] its power in our lives. It could be said to be a reward for the successful completion of a task. It is measured by the difficulty of its completion. W. Clement Stone said something to the effect that what the mind of man believes, man can achieve. This type of achievement is the basis for self confidence. Believe and you may achieve, but action will be required. It is not fair to expect another to believe, that which you only hope for.

DENIAL: *refusal to admit the truth or reality; refusal to acknowledge a person or a thing; negation in logic (nullifying or causing to be ineffective); a psychological defense mechanism in which confrontation with a personal problem, or reality, is avoided by denying the existence of the problem or reality.*

—*Something that "is" in the absence of something real...when fantasy becomes reality.*

One of the more amusing anecdotes[†] of the recovery community, at least here in Arizona, is, "Denial is not the river in Egypt." Denial also is used as an acronym meaning, "Don't even notice I am lying." These are true, if not humorous, examples of denial. Practicing addicts or alcoholics do not usually notice most of the lies they tell. Denial goes beyond telling lies or even believing them. It defies logic and reason. Its living and being in a lie so deep that you can't tell the difference.

What could cause such a state or condition in a normal human being? Many things can and do. Any event that goes beyond a person's ability to rationalize or understand could be dealt with by denial. Denial is really a self serving mental defense that may take over when a person becomes overwhelmed by a situation or event. War has caused denial in men for centuries. Violence causes it every day. Whenever we cannot accept the stark terror, pain, or vileness which we are confronted by, denial may occur. Unaddressed or undiagnosed, denial may be responsible for many psychological disorders.

Denial seldom is "not" seen as a symptom of chemical dependency. It is an obvious symptom of the Chronic[†], most debilitating, phase of dependency. That is not to say that serious denial must always be a symptom of dependency, or that without being in denial, a person cannot be seriously dependent. Denial falls in the cunning and baffling aspect of dependency. Imagine an invisible line dividing use and dependency that a person crosses one day, and months or even years later knows something happened, is not sure what it is, let alone where it occurred or how to reverse it. Lives have been wasted in the futile search for a long ago crossed line; not noticed or felt at the time, never before acknowledged, crossed in reckless flight from personal demons, sometime ago in the past. The easiest way to understand this scenario is denial. There never was a line. I never crossed it. I'm not missing anything. Therefore, I must be O.K. Now leave me alone and I'll be fine. I don't need any help. S'cuse me while I take another toke. S'not funny. S'not a joke.

Examples:

A) I don't have a problem. You're the problem.

B) I only smoke crack or shoot drugs socially.

C) I can quit anytime. I just don't want to.

D) _____

The only way to overcome denial is to face it and explore its origins. This is not easy or quickly accomplished. It is a process of growth and personal research. A sincere desire for balance and self-improvement may open the door to face these unwelcome realizations. I have never seen anyone excited to face these types of deamons or memories, but thoroughness and strength may begin to break down the power of these delusions. Often a trusted guide such as a therapist or doctor familiar with denial may be required, but the initial exploration can come from within. By its very nature self-improvement will lead a person to challenge the things that most interfere with their wholeness. Denial can be debilitating. Seeing it and understanding its power can be freeing.

HONESTY

HONEST: *free from fraud or deception; Legitimate; Truthful; Genuine, Real; Reputable; Respectable.*

—Based in reality.

HONESTY: *fairness and straight forwardness of conduct; adherence to the facts; Sincerity.*

—The facts, just the facts, no foo-foo, just the facts: TRUTH

Honesty is simply the refusal to lie, cheat and steal in any way. It could be described as the absence of glorification. Honesty is the truth of reality as you understand it at the time. As your knowledge of self and life grows, you are more and more capable of honesty. You have developed awareness that give you a base in reality. If you are ill informed or have been deceived, you may be in error and still be totally honest. Honesty is not about right or wrong, it is about what you believe. Honesty requires knowledge. You cannot be honest about something you know nothing about. (Unless, of course, you state that you don't know.) "Know-it-all" is a polite way of saying, "They're not very honest about the limits of their knowledge."

How important is honesty? In dealing with the outside world it would seem a handicap in some instances. Without adequate self-esteem and pride, deceit is almost a mandatory† defense mechanism. If we are totally honest we must present the true nature of ourselves. This would be emotional suicide to some people. Dishonesty by its very nature feeds on itself. The most difficult thing about lies are remembering them. The truth is easy (and often painful) to remember. The most damaging lies are those we tell ourselves.

What if you honestly find yourself unacceptable? Can you change that? When the truth hurts it is usually due to our own unrealistic expectations or denial. If we accept the pain as part of our reality, we become empowered to change ourselves into a more personally acceptable person. This is honesty in action. This is what healthy people practice in everyday life. Lies are not honest. Lies are simply ego enhancers. It would seem then that if you made no definitive statements you would be assured of being honest. It's not quite that simple. What about those quiet times when it is just you, yourself and your soul, when there is no one to talk to but yourself? At these times you have the option to accept reality for what it really is or float through dreamland, i.e. Denial. This scenario has little meaning unless you're dishonest to or about yourself. In our lives it's cleansing to rid ourselves of our denial and be honest. This has to be a process, not an event (immediate change). Everybody has lied to himself or herself. This can become a defense mechanism for low self-esteem or lack of healthy pride. When we believe the lies we tell ourselves it is called denial. When we are in denial, we are out of touch with reality and our decisions are based on the fantasy of the denial, not in the facts of the reality.

That said, what about white lies. What are they? How are they defined and are they acceptable? What constitutes a white lie and differentiates it from what we have determined honesty could be? White lies are told when there is no benefit in telling the truth, and telling it would cause unnecessary pain to another. There can be no personal gain or avoidance of responsibility in a white lie. This is not to say that white lies are acceptable, excusable or necessary. They are definitely not honest. If not kind, they are unnecessary no matter how you rationalize them.

Finally, how about lies of omission? When the truth is relevant[†] to the situation and intentionally omitted, it is a lie of omission. Not mentioning to someone that you are in a relationship, when it could interfere with your intentions, is a lie of omission. "I don't know" is the classic lie of omission. Not saying something to avoid hurting another can be tolerated as a white lie. Not saying something to avoid personal discomfort is a lie of omission.

3

ACTION

(CHOICE)

FEELINGS / EMOTIONS

FEELING: sensitivity; conscious recognition; often-unreasoned opinion or belief; deeply felt.

—**Perception, What you internalize, Response to external stimuli or action. Negated[†] by reactionary attitudes. INTERNALLY DIRECTED -/- SENSE.**

EMOTION; the affective aspect (influence) of consciousness.

—**Internally inspired attitude toward an external thing... what you project. The basis of action. EXTERNALLY DIRECTED -/- BEHAVIOR.**

Everyone has feelings. Some people are more in touch with theirs than others. Feelings are interpretations. What a person is exposed to has an effect on them. This effect is a feeling. Feelings are situational. This experience is unique to the person having it. Many persons may deduce[†] the same feeling from an event, yet each may have a different personal perspective[†]. Feelings can be historically anticipated but will not always be the consistent. Intensity of feelings depends on many factors but is usually directly relevant[†] to the emotions they inspire.

Feelings are learned. The teacher may be experience, a parent, a partner, an organization, etc. There is no end to the lessons of feelings. They are constantly barraging everyone. Some categorize them, process them, and then choose an appropriate action. Others exist in a void of denial, most find themselves somewhere in the middle.

Are feelings powerful? Without the restraints of logic and

knowledge they can ruin lives. Logic gives feelings direction and allows choice. Knowledge widens the variety of feelings and expands the allowable choices. Logic and knowledge may empower a person to control feelings thereby buffering the harmful effects on one's life.

How many feelings are there? How many stars are in the sky? What color is a car? The answers are the same: no one knows for sure. Generally, it doesn't matter unless the answer has an effect on your life. If you are looking for your car it helps to locate it by looking for the color of yours in a crowded parking lot. If you are lost, the position of certain stars may help you find your way. What feelings are present, are the ones you have to be able to identify and understand first. Once you are able to make this distinction you become empowered to expand your basis of feeling and in turn enjoy more personal freedom.

Are feelings good or bad? Some can be either depending on the situation. Usually this determination will inspire a like response or reaction. For the moment let's address negative feelings. Here is a list of some core negative feelings and their definitions.

SAD: affected with or expressive of grief or unhappiness. Thesaurus; adj \ DOWNCAST, MELANCHOLY.
—Low, let down, grief.

LONELY: cut off from others; (solitary), producing a feeling of bleakness or desolation. Thesaurus; adj \ LONE (alone, lonesome, solitary), FORLORN.
—Unheard, isolated.

GUILT: justly chargeable with or responsible for a breach of conduct or crime, justly liable to or

deserving of a penalty.
Thesaurus; adj \ BLAMEWORTHY (account-
able, answerable, responsible).
—**Something you did.**

SHAME: *a condition of humiliating disgrace or*
disrepute, i.e.; character: something to be regret-
ted. Thesaurus; n \ DISGRACE.
—**Something you are.**

FEAR: *an unpleasant, often strong emotion*
caused by anticipation or awareness of danger,
anxious concern, reason for alarm. Thesaurus;
ALARM, AGITATION, DISMAY, FRIGHT,
HORROR, PANIC, DREAD, TERROR, ANXI-
ETY, CONCERN, WORRY.
—**Opposite of faith, afraid.**

PAIN: *to make suffer or cause distress, a basic*
body sensation induced by a noxious stimulus,
received by naked nerve endings, characterized
by physical discomfort and typically leading to
*evasive action. Thesaurus; n \ pang, throe vb *
HURT, ache, suffer.
—**Hurt, anguish, sorrow**

INADEQUATE: *not adequate: insufficient, not*
capable. (Not) ADEQUATE: sufficient for a spe-
cific requirement. (Not) SUFFICIENT: enough
to meet the needs of a situation
Thesaurus; DEFICIENT, defective, incomplete,
lacking, wanting.
—**Not enough.**

These listed feelings are known as primary feelings. They are core feelings that are difficult to break down into others. Most feelings could be classified as compound feelings; that is, two or more primary feelings forming what are referred to as a compound feeling. A good example of this would be "deceived." Deceived, or deception is a very real feeling. It is however not primary. Deception could be a combination of "fear, pain and inadequacy." It could also be a combination of "sad lonely and shame." The point is; that in and of itself, deception is not a primary, but rather a compound feeling. It has been said, as well as argued, that the only feelings there are, are fear and love.

This list of feelings is obviously not complete. What has been attempted is to list the most relevant† negative feelings to the process of recovery. When in a state of desperation or confusion the feelings experienced are seldom pleasant or function inspiring. To the contrary, they are debilitating and restrictive. It seems that acknowledging them would be a form of self mutilation. What good could be gotten from scraping off the scabs of time and denial and reopening these old wounds and terrors? The reality of the situation is that the only rehabilitation from these dysfunctions is acknowledgment and exposing them to the truth in which we would live and thrive. Although this seems incredibility difficult, the rewards of function and strength far overcome and outweigh the effort required.

Emotions are different than feelings. As discussed, feelings are an inwardly directed sense, prompted by external stimuli. Emotions on the other hand are an internally motivated sense, externally directed toward a person, place or thing. The object the emotion is directed "at" may or may not have inspired it. Knowledge of the feeling connected to it is the basis of function and emotional stability. It could be said that emotions are responses to feelings. Note the term response. Response implies† that an intellectual process has occurred. (More about that concept later.) Emotions then, are the motivators of actions.

Emotional problems can usually be defined by: 1) An un-awareness of the link to feelings. 2) An inability to process intellectually or logically the connection to feelings. 3) A powerlessness to act upon, or own, emotions from either situational or personal circumstance. 4) Failure to acknowledge any of the above.

There exists a connection between mental and emotional well-being, the mental being the identification and acknowledgment of feeling, and the emotional being the choice of effect on one's person. This connection of heart and head is imperative to health and wholeness. A break in the sequence instills confusion and doubt, which may lead to "dis-function." The absence of this connection may impair maturity and natural development.

For now let's see how negative emotions inspire negative actions that may result in negative consequences.

SLOTH: disinclination to action or labor: INDO-LENCE†, spiritual apathy† or indifference. Thesaurus; n \ idleness, heedlessness, inattentiveness.
—Laziness.

WRATH: strong vengeful anger or dignation. Thesaurus; n \ ANGER, fury, indignation†.
—Ill will.

COVETOUSNESS: marked by inordinate desire for wealth or possessions of another Thesaurus; adj. \ having or marked by an urgent and often unscrupulous desire for possessions.
—Desire for the possessions of another, Greed, Avarice.

LUST: To have an intense desire or need: CRAVE. Thesaurus; n \ DESIRE, LONG.
—Obsession.

GLUTTONY: excess in eating or drinking, greedy or excessive indulgence. Thesaurus; adj. \ SATIATION, ravenous, piggish, intemperate.
—Too much of anything, more than you need.

ENVY: painful or resentful awareness of an advantage enjoyed by another joined with a desire to possess the same advantage: MALICE. Thesaurus; n \ spiteful malice and resentment over another's advantage.
—Position or opportunities of another.

ARROGANCE (False Pride): an attitude of superiority manifested in an overbearing manner or in presumptuous claims or assumptions an exaggerated sense of self-importance: CONCEIT. Thesaurus; n \ an exaggerated sense of one's own importance, self-importance, loftiness, pompousness, presumptuousness, superiority, bossiness, dominance, high-handedness; condescension, snobbishness, boastfulness, braggadocio, swagger cockiness, smugness, vanity.
—Self-centeredness.

Now that we have explored the difference as well as the connection of feelings and emotions, we have the knowledge necessary to separate them and understand the power they wield. This knowledge has little, if any power unless we implement[†] it into our lives. So far we have defined their negative aspects without considering their opposites. Positive feelings promote positive attitudes or emotions. Let's look first at the definitions of the corresponding positive feelings and their contrast to their negative counterparts.

STRENGTH: *capacity for exertion or endurance, power to resist. IMPREGNABILITY. Thesaurus; n \ sturdiness, toughness, healthiness, soundness.*
—**Internal power, guts.**

HEALING: *to make sound or whole, to restore to health, overcoming an undesirable condition: MEND. Thesaurus; vb \ CURE, remedy.*
—**Letting go.**

COMPASSION: *sympathetic consciousness of others' distress together with a desire to alleviate it. SYMPATHY. Thesaurus; n \ empathy, charity, clemency.*
—**Helpfulness.**

VALUES: *something (as a principal or quality) intrinsically† valuable or desirable. Thesaurus; merit, virtue, revere, reverence, venerate, WORTH.*
—**Personal code of ethics.**

TRUST: *assured reliance on the character, ability or truth of someone or something: dependence on something future or contingent. Thesaurus; confidence, dependence, faith, hope, reliance, RELY ON.*
—**Sticking your neck out.**

FAITH: *firm belief in something for which there is no proof. Thesaurus; n \ BELIEF.*
—**Sticking your neck out all the way.**

WISDOM: *ability to discern, INSIGHT, good sense. Thesaurus; n \ KNOWLEDGE, information, sense, judgment.*
—**Learned power.**

COURAGE: mental or moral strength to venture, persevere, and withstand danger, fear or difficulty. Thesaurus; n \ a quality of mind or temperament that enables one to stand fast in the face of opposition, hardship, or danger.
—Strength to face life.

These primary positive feelings have every bit the power of negative ones. The effects they have on our lives are positive and we would like to hold on to them. Circumstance cannot always be anticipated and negative feelings can overwhelm us and cancel our positive attitudes. It seems that our society[†] expounds more on the negative aspects of itself than the joy that must somewhere be present.

Positive emotions are inspired by good or positive feelings. They usually result in positive responses from others. These are positive emotions we can practice.

DILIGENCE: persevering application, the attention and care expected or required of a person. Thesaurus; industrious, persevering, persistent.
—Seeing things through.

FORGIVENESS: to give up resentment of or claim to requital for, to cease to feel resentment against. Thesaurus; vb \ EXCUSE, pardon
—Letting go.

LIBERALITY: marked by generosity, not literal or strict, giving freely or unstintingly. Thesaurus; openhandedness.
—Benevolence, acceptance.

CHASTITY: purity in conduct and intention, personal integrity. Thesaurus; adj \ free from every trace of the lewd or salacious.
—Rigorous honesty.

ABSTINENCE: voluntary forbearance from an indulgence or craving. Thesaurus; n \ TEMPERANCE, continence, sobriety.
—Doing without.

KINDNESS: a sympathetic or helpful nature, to give pleasure or relief. Thesaurus; adj \ showing or having a gentle considerate manner, TENDERNESS.
—Nice.

HUMILITY: the quality or state of being humble, not proud or haughty : not arrogant or assertive. Thesaurus; adj \ lacking all signs of pride, aggressiveness or self-assertiveness.
—Down to earth, being teachable.

To summarize;
Feelings are a response to external stimuli.
Feelings are a sense, not an action.
Emotions are a response to that sense.
Emotions emerge as an action or attitude.

We can only hope to better understand and process our feelings. We cannot control them. Our emotions, on the other hand, are within our power to determine. When we feel led to a negative place by our feelings, we have the right, power and hopefully the understanding to not proceed. This may be where the phrase, "Forgive and Forget" came from. Realistically, little if any personal growth or good comes from a negative act or attitude. Owning our feelings and not acting on them is often in our best interest. It can provide emotional safety as well as personal growth. If you cannot be positive, process the feelings associated with the situation and take the steps necessary to protect yourself without participating. Often the proper choice of emotions is not to respond at all. Until a thing has an effect on our lives, we don't necessarily need to have an opinion.

RESPONSE / REACTION

RESPONSE: *the activity or inhibition[†] of previous activity of an organism or any of its parts resulting from stimulation; to be answerable;*

> **—A decision to take an action based on identified stimuli...Accountability.**

REACTION: *resistance or opposition to a force, influence or movement, tendency toward a former and usually outmoded political or social order or policy.*

> **—Action without conscience thought. Impulse or Instinct...No Accountability.**

Reactions, as Webster alludes[†], are past experiences replayed in a different time. They may or may not be relevant[†] to the situation at hand. Some reactions are in reality, survival techniques. This fact does not make them either rational or functional. Soldiers are taught reactions as a discipline for war. Without war, what good are they? Some reactions are functional; however, they usually miss a key ingredient in a functional life. That ingredient is thought. To wit: a conscience decision to take an action. People who are reactionary have the excuse of not thinking to explain their behavior. Sadly this rationale is accepted in much of today's world. Accountability is paramount to recovery from any difficulty. Reactions negate[†] accountability and thereby must be avoided in the course of recovery.

To respond one must make a decision, which makes even the least responsible of us somehow part of the equation of the situation. Response takes conscience thought and a following action. This thought is what makes us accountable. This process is what encourages us to develop into more productive, functional people and begins to instill a sense of growth and worth into lives lacking meaning and or direction.

We need to be able to respond to life in order to be responsible. We need to be responsible to have value to ourselves, others or society[†]. Unnecessary reactions are usually inflammatory at best and little, if any, good comes from them. This process of responding can create boundaries and values when discovered, and strength and conviction when incorporated into a recovery-based life.

Addicts and alcoholics, in particular, have drunk and drugged up the luxury to react to life's events. Their lack of judgment and logic has put them in the precarious[†] position of needing to take "full" responsibility for all their actions. With the exception of those who have been force fed these chemicals, they have opted to evade reality by the use of chemicals and relied on reactionary behavior to avoid the consequences of such lifestyles. Your time has run out! Reality is all that is left. New information[†] is necessary in order to instill meaningful change. Change is required to become whole. New behavior, developed by new motivation, is the only road out. If you always do what you always did, you'll always get what you always got. Good luck.

FEEL, THINK, ACT
(PROCESS)

FEEL: *to undergo passive experience of, to have one's sensibilities markedly affected by; Passive: acted upon by an external agency, receptive to outside impressions or influences.*

—**To deduce[†] or determine, as by the above.**

THINK: *to form or have in the mind; to exercise the powers of judgment, conception, or reason.*

—**To determine based on history, logic and/or need.**

ACT: *the doing of a thing. (Something done voluntarily.)*

—**The result of a decision. The conclusion of the process described above.**

What we feel has a major influence on how we think, which in turn has a profound[†] effect on how we act. What inspires this process in you? Do you understand it as a process? Has the actual determination of feeling, the incorporation of intelligent information[†] and the consequent deduction and storage of it, ever been considered?

As discussed earlier, feelings are an internal sense, inspired by external stimuli. The identification and understanding of them are individual and flexible. They are not limited by lack of education[†] or life experiences. They do not come automatically with wealth or privilege. The most sheltered or uneducated may, with dedication and perseverance, have the deepest understanding of them and their power. Their incorporation into one's life must be a choice as forced requirements seldom have an enduring effect on personal growth.

Thinking is a process by which external stimuli is processed internally, and optimally, personally responded to. If it is to be agreed that actions are limited to, as well as determined by, one's capacity to identify feelings, it would be logical to believe that in order to expand the choices of action 1) A capacity to identify and process feelings must be increased, and 2) A wider range of feelings available to act upon must be cultivated.

Actions are the beginning of future consequences as well as the consequence for past ones. They are unavoidable. The result of them may be often predicted or even looked forward to. An action repeatedly rehearsed can be fine tuned to perfection. Athletes and artists must develop their abilities through repeated actions. A factory or construction worker must learn certain manual actions to become proficient in their job. Teachers or office workers must utilize certain actions to be competent in their occupation. Even criminals master certain actions to not get caught. For sure, actions thought through are usually the more successful as well as functional.

Imagine feelings as the motor that powers our lives. The more efficient, powerful and versatile feeling identification becomes, the better our lives function. When maintained and improved upon, identifying feelings becomes a driving force. Thoughts are like maps. A map gives perspective[†], direction and allows for planning. Without a map, destinations are dreams, not accomplishments. Direction is irrelevant without perspective. Unless you know where you are going, how will you know when you've arrived, or what to expect? You can't drive to Hawaii. Action is movement. Feeling and thought are control. Without control, chaos reigns and a train wreck is inevitable[†]. To become reasonably predictable, actions must be powered by feeling and directed by thought. A broad knowledge base, and the ability to utilize it, is a powerful and important resource in life. In an ideal environment this dynamic is the basis for all growth.

Fact 1

Feelings are a response to people, places and or things as they affect your current reality. The process of understanding feelings is a measure of mental capacity. Limited knowledge of feelings, and the influence they have on reality, greatly restricts options available to process them. More amazing perhaps is the fact that feelings are unique to the individual, and only that particular person has ultimate control over the effectiveness of processing them into thought.

Fact 2

Thinking is a process, which culminates in a decision. It is most often inspired by feelings, which, when processed, are a result of personal knowledge and opinions of oneself. It is the process whereby feelings become actions. Thinking is not determined by education†, although education may broaden the base of thought. Thinking depth is a result of experiences and the intellectual ability to recall them. Thought response is conditioned by self-knowledge, expectations and understanding of feelings. It can only be limited by denial of the possibility of change.

Fact 3

Actions are responses to thoughts (thinking), based on feelings processed and or denied. To live a functional life one must learn to identify feelings, process them intellectually and emotionally, then determine not only the logical, but also the functional action to take, if any, based on a value system. Sometimes not taking an action is the best decision available. Practiced and studied, functional decisions and actions cannot only lead to a productive existence; it can be the most empowering aspect of change available today.

Feelings = *motor and fuel (power).*

Thoughts = *map and perspective*[†] *(direction).*

Actions = *movement and change (consequences).*

INTEGRITY

INTEGRITY: firm adherence to a code of especially moral or artistic values; Incorruptibility: an unimpaired condition; Soundness: the quality or state of being complete or undivided; Completeness. See Honesty.

—**Strength of your convictions. How consistently you act.**

Integrity is a personal trait, learned and developed. It is your personal code of conduct. You can to measure your integrity by your values, but without values you can have no integrity. An awareness and development of values will become integrity if it is morally grounded and consciously adhered to. Discovery of an individual's values, based on the justness of their beliefs, will determine the degree of integrity they develop. Integrity can open or close doors of opportunity, based on our core beliefs.

The incorruptibility of integrity has no societal significance. It is an inner-personal guide to actions and beliefs which may change circumstantially. Without knowledge of integrity there is nothing to evaluate our actions and thoughts in everyday life. It is the measure of our convictions. Integrity is moral strength in action. Changes are inevitable. As one's life evolves, or changes, integrity must also change to reflect the new information received.

Commitment to your belief system is your integrity. It is not contingent on anyone else's. It is determined by a person, his or her history, knowledge and values. The depth of conviction measures its strength. Integrity is personal, progressive and strengthening. Our integrity is defined by our boundaries and is only as strong as our commitment to the values and moral character that it is based on. Our esteem and self-worth is how we develop it and our honesty is dependent on it. Integrity tips the scale of moral decision making and guides us to right action. It develops consistency in our actions and gives credibility to our decisions.

Integrity enhances our person. It instills confidence in our decisions, justness in our actions, and conviction to our beliefs. Integrity allows us to believe in ourselves, knowing that if we maintain a balance of justice and mercy, all will be at least rationally understandable. If we achieve this balance, we realize the serenity of it. Integrity can be defined only in the depth of conviction a person has in their core self. The power of one's integrity is relative only to that person. I cannot have integrity for you, nor can you have mine. It's the ultimate inside job.

VALUES

VALUES: something (as a principal or quality) intrinsically[†] desirable; to consider or rate highly.
—What you believe in. Justifiable principals.

Values are the foundation of our lives. Without a basis for what we stand for, or on, we cannot achieve real stability. We must be knowledgeable of our values lest they not accord us the ability to build a functional life upon them. They have as much strength as we have commitment to them. They are rigid by design, yet flexible by nature. They don't always work for our friends or even family, the only requirement is that they work for us.

There are four types of values: societal, modeled, experiential and experimental. Societal are those accepted by the society[†] that one lives in. They are the basis for the rules that govern a group. They are necessary for order and *cohesion*. Modeled values are those observed in other people or societies, and adapted to out of attraction. Experiential values are those that a person has knowledge of, but not necessarily internalized or adapted their own life. Societal values may be experiential values if they have been imposed on a person without their personal adaptation. Experimental values are those sought out, studied, analyzed, understood and implemented[†] to enhance one's life.

Societal values are imposed values. Webster defines society as "A voluntary association of individuals for common ends: especially an organized group working together because of common interests." For example, values in a prison type society should be much different than those in a functional loving family. If a person from such a family should find themselves incarcerated, they would have to adjust their values in order to exist. The function of a society, or family, is determined by the strength of its values and the compliance of its members. Secular religions differ widely in the basis for their societal values and most demand compliance at the risk of eternal misgiving for failure to do so. Peer groups of all kinds develop societal value systems that require adaptation for continued acceptance.

Modeled values are those, which are observed in others. A value that is present in another person or society may be copied if merit is seen in it. If a need exists in a family, society or a person that is, or could be, attributed[†] to the lack of a value that is obvious in another situation, it may be modeled in hopes of achieving the same result. As a rule, modeled values are adapted and adjusted to fit an individual intention. Modeled values are not usually demanded, they are determined to be desirable.

Experiential values are those that have been experienced either in person or as a member of a group. They are not necessarily understood personally and may not be appropriate in a current situation. Basic knowledge is not sufficient to implement[†] these types of values; however that knowledge may be adequate enough to begin the process of their creation and influence. Many family values are experiential in that they have always been utilized but have never been implemented[†] in one's personal life. The old adage comes to mind, "Just because you grow up on a ranch, doesn't mean you know how to ride a horse."

Finally there are experimental values. In the absence of, or in lieu of, these previous kinds of values, are we to be limited to those values that have been determined to have worth by those who have preceded us? I don't think so! Once the importance of values is understood and acknowledged in one's life, when personal awareness of the lack of values, or the painful knowledge that those being practiced are incongruent[†], experimental values are an option. It is at this point that we go on a search, or quest, to understand our value system. Without knowledge we have no direction. Without direction, life has no meaning. Without meaning, we have no values. Without values, we have no life. Etc, etc, etc. This type of value is discovered and implemented[†] on a trial and error basis.

Values are important and obtainable. Dedication to and practice of them will promote personal growth. Even if the values practiced today are someone else's, the understanding of their power in directing our lives will be beneficial. It is hoped that the discovery[†] of their importance will instill a need to understand and implement[†] a system of functional values, to be the foundation of our futures.

The following is a list of basic values. Values are not people, places or things. They relate to feelings and emotions at the same time. They are the foundations of what we stand for or against. They define our boundaries and clarify our beliefs. Without them we are doomed.

SUGGESTED VALUES

LOYALTY	*commitment*	1-2-3-4-5-6-7-8-9-10
RESPONSIBILITY	*personal accountability*	1-2-3-4-5-6-7-8-9-10
HUMILITY	*non-judgmental*	1-2-3-4-5-6-7-8-9-10
HONESTY	*truthfulness*	1-2-3-4-5-6-7-8-9-10
OPEN-MINDEDNESS	possibility of change	1-2-3-4-5-6-7-8-9-10
WILLINGNESS	open to change	1-2-3-4-5-6-7-8-9-10
COMPASSION	caring	1-2-3-4-5-6-7-8-9-10
CONSIDERATION	respect	1-2-3-4-5-6-7-8-9-10
SPIRITUALITY	intrinsic rightness	1-2-3-4-5-6-7-8-9-10
FAITH	believing without seeing	1-2-3-4-5-6-7-8-9-10
VIRTUE	morality	1-2-3-4-5-6-7-8-9-10
Other	_____	1-2-3-4-5-6-7-8-9-10

Armed with this basic understanding of values, how does one determine if their personal values are adequate for their life? What determines the functionality of an individual's personal values?

_____

_____

_____

_____

YES / NO   Do you understand your values?

YES / NO   Are you willing to defend your values?

YES / NO   Do you feel comfortable with your values?

YES / NO   Do people respect your values?

YES / NO   Do you respect your values?

YES / NO   Does your social environment support your values?

REMEMBER:

- Understanding values does not implement† them in one's life.
- No two people have identical values.
- People may share values, but utilize them to different degrees.
- Situationally, values may define the course of a circumstance or relationship.
- Values alone will not give life balance.
- Having values will not cure addiction.
- Understanding, maintaining and practicing values is empowering.
- Values change.

BOUNDARIES

BOUNDARY: *something that indicates or fixes a limit or extent.*

— *What lengths a person will abide or tolerate.*

What are these magical limitations and why are they important? How do they define who we are? To begin, let's understand that everyone has boundaries. From the most structured goody-two-shoes, to the wildest craziest most irresponsible people, all of them have boundaries. Boundaries are part of living, part of our personalities. Without them we could not exist. It would be like letting go of the steering wheel on the exit ramp of a freeway. They protect us from the world and even ourselves. Often they protect the world from us. A boundary can be rigid, invisible, or anywhere in between. Knowledge of boundaries empowers us to control and shape them to our greatest use. I believe there to be three main types of personal boundaries; Impenetrable, Healthy, and Not-Yet.

Impenetrable boundaries are rigid, immovable. They are a necessity in some instances. In times of grave peril or extreme confusion they provide a safe haven. Too often in this day and age people have a tendency to hide from life behind these types of boundaries. These people find themselves alone in their self-imposed exile. Unable to communicate to the world from behind their rigidity, they become susceptible to many forms of manipulation[†].

Healthy boundaries are flexible based on circumstance. There are numerous kinds of them. We all should have at least physical, sexual, intellectual and emotional (spiritual) ones. The physical ones define our personal space and whom we allow inside. They establish when and how we are touched and by whom. Our sexual boundaries limit where and how we will be sexual, and with whom. Intellectual boundaries determine what we believe. Without them we are vulnerable to any line of "B.S." Perhaps the most important boundary of all is emotional. An emotional boundary distinguishes an individual. It keeps a person from taking on the problems of the world. It defines what a person feels and separates it from other's feelings. Of all four kinds, emotional boundaries are the most personal. They are about a person and their history. Feelings thoughts and decisions are all that matter within emotional boundaries. If there is balance here, there is balance in life. Unresolved issues always find a foundation within emotional boundaries.

Our boundaries are constantly being tested. Other people continually test our limits without necessarily being aggressive. In order to understand our position in a group, or in life for that matter, we must know where we stand. Our boundaries, and the affects of our associates upon them, determine this. The key to having healthy boundaries is understanding them. The key to understanding life is in emotional boundaries.

"I don't do that sort of thing" is a boundary. "I'll try it," is a boundary too. They are your personal limits. Boundaries define who and what we are. If "I" were to know your boundaries, I would have an idea what kind of person you are. If "you" do not know your boundaries, I could have a great deal of manipulative power over you. Boundaries can provide a great deal of protection for us or allow a great deal of deception to us. They protect us from being misled into directions we don't want to go. If we do not understand them we can be in dangerous places before we realize it. Boundaries require a persistent inventory† taking of our surroundings and the people present. Life is not constantly the same and neither are our boundaries. As life changes, our boundaries reflect the change. The more danger or pain we feel, the more rigid our boundaries become. True insanity could be described as a total absence of boundaries.

HUMILITY

HUMILITY: the quality or state of being humble.

HUMBLE: not proud or haughty, not arrogant or assertive; reflecting, expressing, or offered in a spirit of deference or submission.
— *The absence of ego. A teachable state.*

Humility is not taking or giving, it's not an act or a tool. Humility is an inside job. It is connecting with that inner part of yourself and being "OK" with what is there. Humility is the personification of the connection between heart and head. It is a cyclic† by-product of serenity. Without humility there can be no inner harmony.

People don't look humble. They act humble, either by word or deed. Humility is not a natural state. People want to be acknowledged. Attracting that interest is not humble. Often the person who deserves the most attention is the most humble. When not acknowledged, they accept it with grace and dignity. These people do not do or say things for acknowledgement anyway. Acknowledgement from others is not as important to them as the connection they have achieved, and the peace they have found within themselves.

When a connection is made between your dreams and your reality, and you find the inner harmony of that connection, humility is an option. If a situation does not affect you, or has no affect on your life, humility can be a blessing. It helps to keep you centered and gives reason not to participate in others chaos.

Humility cannot be given or received, it either is or it is not. It is searched for and developed, not bought or found. When true humility is achieved it could be described as knowing what we really are, without consideration for that which we wish to be. It is temporary at best. The cycles of life, vocation and relationships, have a weakening effect on our inner selves. Serenity fades and humility follows. Sometimes being ignored can be a blessing.

Humility is keeping your mouth shut about yourself. It is not giving comparison credence[†]. It's allowing others their lives, and sometimes getting out of their way. It is not being slighted or trod upon, endures no abuse or manipulation[†]. Humility is accepting your life, no fanfare, and no promotion. If you cannot do that, no amount of power, sex or money can bring you happiness. Humility is a perfect partner with serenity. It's harmony within the universe.

RE-UNIFICATION

(WILLINGNESS)

AUTHORITY

AUTHORITY: persons in command.
—Rule makers and / or enforcers.

The first thing that must be understood about authority is that it requires an amount of responsibility. The greater the authority, the larger the responsibility. Without responsibility, authority becomes insolence†. True authority could be described as a benevolent† dictator. A justness and consideration tempered with rigid guidelines. Without authority there would be chaos. Intimidation would reign and our society† would vanish. In no way do I mean to imply that a great amount of authority is necessary. If people acted in a responsible, cooperative manner, there would be less need for as much authority as we now endure. Authority often infringes on our freedoms. Our freedoms often infringe on another person's. It is at times like these that we feel affronted by authority.

CAPTIVE AUTHORITY

Whenever a portion of our time is controlled by another could be classified as captive authority. A great deal of diplomacy may be required in these instances. This could be attributed† to the fact that most people would rather not be there. A student, during those marvelous early spring days, might be a good example. In the absence of a level of maturity which allows for delaying gratification, a captive type of environment is required to maintain a learning atmosphere. It takes a level of obedience as well as respect to accept this type of authority. Without some degree of acceptance, people would simply leave this type of situation and do as they wish. Often the primary acceptance is that the person subject to the authority needs to attend this function for personal gain or to avoid undesirable consequences. For example; if a person does not attend school, they will not be taught what is necessary to graduate. If they do not graduate they will not be able to get a good paying job. On the same note, if a person does not go to work regularly, they may be passed up for promotions or raises. Attendance does not guarantee that a person's supervisor will be a fair or rational authoritarian. Attendance without compliance is no better though.

FAMILY AUTHORITY

In a family setting, if no one is in a position of authority, nothing seems to get accomplished. A great problem in our society today is the absence and/or abuse of this concept. Too often siblings are made to be "too" responsible for younger family members. Before being given enough knowledge to fully understand their position, they are forced into an authoritarian position over others. Those in charge sometimes "bully" those they are responsible for. This could be the result of many dynamics. The most common, I have found, is resentment by the authoritarian, who has not had time to mature before being forced to be responsible for siblings, who have not received proper guidance or discipline. I hear a giant sucking sound when I envision this scenario. Youth's wonder and magic being swallowed up by premature responsibility, "Down the drain like a lukewarm bath". Another generation left to germinate itself. Teenagers today are the second generation of this type of regerminated dysfunction. If this cycle is not broken, our society will require more and more authority until we no longer have the ability to make any decisions for ourselves.

SOCIAL AUTHORITY

Social authority is simply what is best for the "most" people. These are the rules we live by in society. Generally they are flexible and just for the benefit of all. In time of war or great disaster rigid authority may be required to prevent chaos. Prisoners are subjected to extreme, rigid authority. Convicts would rather be almost anywhere else. They have usually done something to violate another person's freedom. Generally they have not obeyed social authority. Incarceration is a consequence of this type of behavior. It is the most severe consequence short of death in our society. Incarceration is supposed to be a period of confinement as punishment. It was decided not long ago to forgo the punishment in favor of rehabilitation. Generally the education† people receive in prison is, "how not to get caught next time." Respect for authority is a foreign concept in prison. Intimidation is the rule rather than the exception. Upon release convicts must re-adapt to life in society. Without this "adaptation" they usually return to incarceration.

DELEGATION OF AUTHORITY

This act, delegation†, passes authority to another. The responsibility of the authority is also being passed to the receiver. It is not "bad" or "wrong" to refuse this responsibility. Often delegation is misused to cover up or shift the responsibility of an action before the consequences are apparent. (A.K.A. "Cover Your Butt") Authority must at times be delegated. The principal of a school cannot teach every class. The president of a corporation cannot do every job. The holders of these positions must delegate authority. They knowingly pass responsibility when delegating authority. If the person accepting the authority cannot also accept the responsibility, the whole dynamic turns into a house of cards. Much can be said about authority and its obvious abuses in today's world. The main point

I am attempting to make is, be sure you are responsible when using authority, and do not accept the responsibility for someone else's sinking ship. Be your own person and act as responsible as the situation allows.

RESPECT OF AUTHORITY

I am not an expert on respect of authority. I ask too many questions. One of my favorite bumper stickers reads, "Question Authority." To give authority respect is to give it consideration. To consider it would mean to question it. Most people have a basic fairness about life that lends itself to function. This fairness would allow me to have a certain amount of respect for that person's authority. Aside from consideration, I believe respect for authority to have a certain amount of voluntary compliance or conformity. This willingness[†] to accept another person's direction does not make one weak or easily manipulated. This team concept is mandatory[†] to maintain order in society. Justness would be ideal; unfortunately, it's not always the case. The good of the masses often takes precedence over the rights of a few. Respect is a choice. A choice requires decision. You decide what is best for you as well as society. If you are honest and fair, there should be few problems.

ACCEPTANCE

ACCEPTANCE: *the act of accepting, fact of being accepted; approval.*
—Being "OK".

Acceptance is a natural human need. No matter what we feel about ourselves, we strive for it in many ways. Everyone needs the acceptance of someone. The writer needs acceptance from their critics or they would not be published. The artist needs acceptance of their works or they fail to sell. The baby needs acceptance of their family or they die. In the same way as the baby we need the acceptance of our friends or we die emotionally.

At a time in my life I claimed no friends. I achieved acceptance through negative and destructive means. If our manner of living is unacceptable to those around us, we tend to search out others whose lifestyle will tolerate ours. When this fails we tend to look for acceptance for what we do, or have, rather than who we are. This can start a pattern of dysfunction that can last a lifetime. If we have not learned socially acceptable behaviors, we strive for notice with actions or possessions. We may be able to create a world where all that matters is what we have, or what we are able to do. What happens when such a world unravels, chaos and discontent? Certainly not comfort and understanding! It became clear to me that although I could change cars, houses, girlfriends or cities, wherever I went, I was there. Nothing was rational. Nothing made sense. It was at this point of knowledge that I found myself unacceptable.

If we can take healthy pride in whom and what we are, we are much less likely to feel unacceptable. Peer pressure is less intimidating when the dynamics of acceptance are understood. We are responsible for our acceptability. When our standards of behavior can be maintained, they have a positive effect on our lives. This requires knowledge and dedication. It is not information[†] that can be purchased or taught. It must be searched for and discovered within us. How our standards of life developed, as well as what they mean, is part of our individual histories. We can tell our futures by looking at the past and "not" changing anything. If we find ourselves acceptable, we are probably reasonably happy. If not, what other people think probably has a great deal of power over our inner selves.

Acceptance has a great deal to do with self-esteem or the degree of your belief in yourself. Without this confidence in one's self, people are easy prey for those who would use them for personal gain. It's usually the case that the victimizer uses the victim to bolster[†] his or her own lack of esteem. It is almost always the case that the victimizer is also a victim. Self-esteem cannot be achieved at another's expense. Many people's lives have become a never-ending cycle of being robbed of their esteem, then robbing others of theirs. A healthy person's esteem is based on the "facts" of their accomplishments, not the rewards of them. Esteem is how you play the game, not the final score. Paradoxically[†], winners can be losers while losers win. Acceptance is not a judgment so much as a feeling. It does, of course, entail judgment, but you may be deemed acceptable when you don't feel so. This out of placeness with life leads many to escape into dysfunctional lifestyles. These journeys are often dangerous to the traveler as well as their associates. Eventually, they all lead back to the premise "YOU'VE NOWHERE TO GO THAT YOU WON'T BE."

Types Of Acceptance

	Acceptable	*Not Acceptable*
PERSONAL	success	ineffectiveness
PEER	equality	arrogance
FAMILY	elder respect	abuse
INTELLECTUAL	knowledge	know it all
SPIRITUAL	personal conviction	demanding
FINANCIAL	hard work	over spending or miserliness
SEXUAL	mutual	abuse
PROFESSIONAL	respect	greed
PHYSICAL	reasonable fitness	gluttony
MORAL	kindness	rudeness

This inventory[†] of acceptability may be useful in discovering what you require to feel accepted. By looking at your examples you should be able to see a general picture of what kind of person you are. It will at least give you a sense of what is important to you in life. When something unacceptable is happening in our presence or to us personally, we have options. To know what these options are we must understand our boundaries. This list should show you at least the outer limits of what you find acceptable. This will constantly change[†] as you gather knowledge and experience.

YESTERDAY / TODAY /
TOMORROW

Three days, how important are they? What is their significance? How do they relate to each other? I believe these to be the most influential† days of our lives. It has become clear to me that today is not only the aftermath of yesterday, but also more importantly the foundation of tomorrow.

My life was once a chorus of self-will. I was totally self-absorbed, narcissistic† you might say. In this sociopathic† state, you didn't matter unless you had something I desired. What I desired was rarely moral or functional, thereby, if you had it, you probably were not either. To look for the good in a person such as I was, is an exercise in futility†. I could act nice for a time, but soon my true colors showed through. Needless to say, I didn't stay around anyone or anyplace for long. There was a method in my madness. If you knew what I knew about me, you would not stay long either. Leaving was easier than trying to explain. No commitment, No future, "No-Problem." I became a taker of things and a user of people. Life was a tornado of dysfunction and I had been swept into a vortex† of fantasy. No way out meant "No Hope".

May 5th, 1982 is a day I will always remember. It became my turning point. A person asked me, "What kind of day do you expect to have?" I responded, "Something bad is sure to happen." I had conditioned myself by my beliefs and actions to expect failure, pain and deceit. In my most aggressive intimidating manner I asked him, "What kind of day do you expect to have!" He smiled inquisitively and said, "Don't know, it just started. I'm just gonna do the best I can with the hand I'm dealt and hope the game doesn't end today." He explained in very

simple terms that yesterday wasn't too bad, better than he deserved, if the truth were known. Of course he explained, he was
the only one who really knew "his" truth. He just wanted to get
through today with one good thought to carry into tomorrow.
He could look back to yesterday, tomorrow, and have something good to reflect on. "I'm not sure I understand," I said.
He smiled and said, "I know you don't." After what seemed an
eternity of silence he asked softly, "Want me to explain?"

My knee-jerk reaction was to say something foul and leave.
The problem was that I did not want to go, not just yet. This
guy seemed to have an insight into my soul and for some reason I wanted to hear him out. "Shoot," I said. "Sit down and
have a cup of coffee," he said, "It's not the best, but it's better
than some." He explained that he once felt that the world was
closing in on him and the only solace he could find was at the
bottom of a bottle. He said he never did any drugs, but only
because they were never in his world. Said he expected each
day to be worse than the last and had nearly given up on trying from the pain of failing. He had ruined his life and that of
his kids because he never understood a few simple rules. First,
he explained, nothing is anybody's fault. It just is and if your
there, you are a part of it. So quit judging, cause people who
judge don't matter, and people who matter don't judge. Second,
you're responsible for everything you do, say or even think. So
be kind and sooner or later kindness will be your just reward.
Third, he stressed, never demand justice. People like him could
only hope for mercy. If lady justice weren't blind he'd be long
buried. "Any questions", he asked. I couldn't speak; I just stared
at him with what must have been an imbecilic look. "It'll be
okay if you just breathe," he said, "Go do something nice for a
stranger, just for the sake of being nice." I spent the day in a fog
reflecting on what he had said, his words shooting holes in all
my rationalizations and excuses.

The next morning bright and early I returned to the place

I had met him and waited for about an hour before he came strolling in. In that time I talked to some other people. They all spoke very highly of this guy and assured me that he was a straight up guy who would not lead me astray. He smiled when he saw me and waved. "What'd you do good yesterday?" he asked. It suddenly overwhelmed me that I had done "my" thing for so long that I did not consciously know how to do good things without expecting something in return. In my best bravado tone, I tried to explain this. He smiled and said, "Keep coming back. You'll figure it out. Might take some practice though."

He said today was just time. Twenty-four hours was all. No more, no less. What we do with it is all we can hope to have. There's no Lotto in life. It's just life, and if we do it well, life will reflect that. We cannot go back into yesterday and change† it. We can only do today different and hope for a different result. He said that if I could just figure out how to have one good day without using or abusing anyone, including myself, I would begin to understand. He assured me that it only took a little effort to not want. The things we want are not usually things that we need anyway. If I could do this deal for just today, I would at least have one day of my life that I did not owe anybody for. That sounded good…not easy.

Tomorrow will come, like it or not. Today will become a yesterday. In that mystical† moment of changing, lives can alter their course. He said that he expects every day to be full of challenges to health and happiness. He was not obsessed with winning the game, just intent on staying in it. If he can look back on yesterday without regret, he said, he has a lot more options for today. Life is half what you expect, and half what you deserve, he claimed, and if you do it right you deserve to be happy, joyous and free. "Let yesterday be over, come back tomorrow, and don't forget to do something good today."

1982 was a long time ago, many yesterday's ago. I have

worked diligently to have a functionally successful life. Well intended trial and error has taught me that if I can look back at yesterday with a minimum of sorrow, I have a greater opportunity to be free today. What I am currently doing sets the stage for tomorrow's new adventures. Looking forward without major fear allows me to be a reasonably happy man.

EGO / PRIDE

EGO: *the self especially as "contrasted" with another self or the world.*

—*What you want the world to believe about you.*

PRIDE: *a "reasonable or justifiable" self-respect; delight or elation "arising from" some act, possession, or relationship.*

—*What you know to be true about yourself.*

The understanding of the true meaning of these words is the foundation of implementing[†] their power in your life. As was explained in the foreword, "Knowledge is Power", by understanding these words we become empowered by them. The image we portray to the world needs a basis in fact or we spend too much time attempting to justify it. If what we know to be true about ourselves is not acceptable to our outside world, we can take no true pride in it. As we become more grounded in our lives, we come to an understanding of the rights we have as living beings to become functional persons. Function is dependent on balance. Balance is never constant; it is always in a state of change[†].

Ego / Pride in balance is simply, "What you see is what you get!" When our ego supports our pride in a mirroring way, we are comfortable and confident. Our pride confirms and protects our ego. We know what we appear to be is based in reality. We have few secrets. We have discretion in the details we share and with whom we share them. We are what we appear to be. Self-respect grows. This is a precarious[†] balance and much effort is required to achieve it. Maintaining it creates healthy self-esteem. Esteem is based on the facts of your accomplishments, not in the rewards of them.

Egos are fragile only when they are not supported by pride. When ego outweighs pride, pride becomes overwhelmed. When this imbalance occurs we become captives of our egos. It's like telling a lie. We create an illusion. Energy is spent trying to keep it believable. We can easily let this illusion become our reality and lose contact with our true selves. If what we are hiding is not acceptable to us, our self-respect suffers. Without this respect we have little self-esteem. Pride is based in reality. Reality, like balance, varies. This continual changing requires constant attention. It is too easy, and convenient, to present a front of what we want others to see and ignore those things that we are. When the front we present to the world is not the same as what we know to be true, we are in a state of distress, emotionally first and then physically. We take on the personality of our ego and deny ourselves the independence of reality. We may present a tough image on the outside and feel powerless as a person inside. Some people's egos present a soft, almost docile image, when inside they seethe with rage.

If these depictions bring about discomfort to you, you may ask, "What are our choices?" 1) We lower our standards to become more acceptable to ourselves, (Alter our reality.) 2) We lose confidence in ourselves and often become victims of our fantasy worlds (Abandon our reality.) 3) We learn who we are and take measures to strengthen ourselves so that lies are no longer needed (Accept our reality.) None of these choices seem easy or immediate. The point of all this is that we alone are responsible for the balance of our lives. Others may assist, but it is our life at risk!

WILLINGNESS

WILLING: *inclined or favorably disposed in mind; Ready: prompt to act or respond: Of or relating to the will or power of choosing.*

—Power or belief behind making a decision.

Willingness is a desire, more than an option. If I am willing to eat no menu is required. Without the willingness to eat, a menu is inconsequential[†]. Options do not matter until a decision has been made and action taken. The options then become viable[†] as they relate to the situation. Our choice of action comes with consequences. Willingness does not come with rewards or penalties, it is merely an intention.

Willingness to change[†] is an acknowledgment of the need for change. If all is well and working to its optimum, why on earth would we want to change it? It is only at times when all is "not" right that people look forward to change. Change is facing fear. When the pain of your reality exceeds the fear of the unknown, you will change. The biggest obstacle to willingness is this "fear" of the unknown. It is not like buying a new car. That is an option you have when you become willing to quit trying to fix the broken one in your driveway. Can't afford a new one? How much will an acceptable one cost? How much do you have? None of these questions matter if you are not willing to change vehicles. Sometimes it is easier to just be willing to take a bus. Is a car the problem or is transportation?

Willingness to change is a combination of choice and surrender. Until a person can admit that their course of life needs altering, and the sum of their knowledge is inadequate to arbitrate[†] this change, they have little if any reason to truly trust that any appreciable change is possible. Only when the total of their knowledge to date is obviously, to them, incapable of causing a meaningful alteration to the reality they have come to believe, is willingness worth pursuing.

It is true that willingness in and of itself is worthless without action. Being willing to work has no consequence unless I look for a job. It is almost a paradox[†] that something so important to life has so little value without a following action. It is reminiscent of making a decision…without further action it has no merit.

GUILT / SHAME?

GUILT: *the fact of having committed a breach of conduct, especially violating law and involving a penalty; broadly: guilty conduct; the state of one who has committed an offense especially consciously; feelings of culpability especially for imagined offenses or from a sense of inadequacy; Self-reproach; a feeling of culpability for offenses.*

—I "did" something wrong.

SHAME: *a painful feeling caused by consciousness of guilt, shortcoming, or impropriety; the susceptibility† to such emotion; a condition of humiliating disgrace or disrepute; Ignominy: something that brings censure or reproach; also: something to be regretted; Pity: "it's a shame you can't go"; a cause of feeling shame.*

—I "am" something wrong.

Guilt by association! Have you ever been judged guilty of believing or acting a certain way because of the company you keep? Too bad! Lions do not run with hyenas, nor do straight people run with druggies. What would be the use? What would they have in common? An old saying states, "Apples don't fall too far from the tree." If you have standards, you associate with other people who share the same beliefs. If the people you are associating with have different beliefs, there must be another attraction for you." How strong is this "other" attraction? Do you have a choice? Is this "other" attraction a source of guilt or shame? In the case of a dependent person, these types of associations are usually dysfunctional. People who don't feel O.K.

with themselves have always attracted each other. They look for acceptability from each other (outside sources) to feel O.K. inside. This dynamic of outward acceptance creates co-dependency and leaves the participant subject to the shame of association. If the person giving you validity through acceptance is a drug user, you as an individual have a responsibility to them to condone their drug use. If you do not accept their drug use, you are guilty of not being in acceptance of them.

Guilt is a conscious feeling. It is caused by something you have done, or have participated in, not being acceptable to you. Everyone has been guilty of something. All people have done wrong things. When these "wrong" things become acceptable to a person, they feel shame. They have become a part of the problem, no longer just an observer. Guilt helps a person maintain feelings of self-worth. When confronted with actions that a healthy person finds unacceptable, that person will attempt to effect change. If this change cannot be initiated, we may feel shame for our part in the action, or we may remove ourselves from it so as not to participate any further. If we stay, we pay. Either emotional, physically or financially, we must own our part in any action we participate in.

Shame is a much less conscious feeling than guilt and therefore is much harder to identify. Much is being written about shame these days. Toxic shame is the current bane to mankind. Healthy shame seems too hard to define. It seems always to lead to the toxic variety. Is there a simple explanation for shame? Can shame have such a serious effect on lives that it creates dysfunction? Left unattended, shame can develop into a debilitating and serious issue. Unaddressed shame is often seen best from another's perspective†. This other perspective may open new avenues of change that were previously unknown. An outside observer, helping to discover shame type issues, must be trustworthy and respected. They must be removed from the issue far enough to have a realistic and non-defensive stance.

This work is difficult and enlightening. It is a conscious decision to identify and alleviate a sub-conscious malady. Shame is especially toxic when used as a control mechanism. "I'm ashamed of you," could be a very toxic statement. Being a value judgment, it may not be. The effect that such a statement has on a person determines both the toxicity and the validity of it. Toxically it infers that the accused has no choice but to continue such actions as prompted the statement. In a healthy sense, the same statement may urge a young child to stop wiping "buggers" on furniture. Such an action may be shameful to an adult while a logical solution to a child. If an adult were to have a "snot-worm" hanging from their nose, they would feel shame when it was brought to their attention. The shame would vanish upon correcting the condition. No one walks around knowingly with spaghetti on their shirt; their pants "fly" open. These are sources of healthy shame. While they are happening, we feel shame. When they are rectified, the shame disappears.

What about a situation where we do not see a way to rectify or fix the source of our shame? The first question we must ask ourselves is "Whose shame is this?" "Did I do something wrong, or am "I" something wrong?" Healthy people often approach such questions from the perspective† of, "Compared to what, or, according to whom?" This is not necessarily denial or rationalization. Healthy self-confidence (not arrogance) and self-esteem (not ego) refutes† such dynamics and counters them with statements such as, "I regret having done that, and it was not the right action to have taken." This honest response and not repeating the behavior that it was referring to, establishes the fact that although this particular person did do something unacceptable, they have accepted accountability for the action and do not intend to repeat it.

FEAR

FEAR: *an unpleasant often strong emotion caused by an anticipation or awareness of danger: anxious concern.*

—Overwhelmed by dark intensity.

Fear is intense. It is either motivating or debilitating. It can be a Godsend or the Antichrist. Fear can save or kill us depending on the situation and our personality. It can overcome obstacles or create them. By its very nature, fear is either good or bad and holds no middle ground.

Fear is one of the greatest motivators. It can prompt us to accomplish great things. It urges us to action beyond our comfort level. It instills courage against formidable foes. Fear of loss can give a mother the strength to lift a car from their child, a child to behave before respect is learned, and an addict to take chances not worth taking to maintain their addiction. Fear of not being accepted is core to many dysfunctions. Fear of rejection is probably more motivating to unhealthy dependency than anything else. One of the keys to recovery† is, "Recovering persons need to associate with persons to whom the behavior being abused is understood but 'not' acceptable."

Fear can hold us back from things we need to deal with, such as addiction and self-respect. This deer in the headlight paralysis has caused many situations to end tragically. The power of fear is immense in limiting our options in life. It can make the unthinkable acceptable, the acceptable common, and the common destructive. Fear can become a way of life instead of a force in it. This generally begins a chain of events which almost always ends in disaster, shame, guilt and forced accountability.

Fear can promote great accomplishments in ordinary people. It can keep great people from realizing their worth let alone their greatness. Fear plays no favorites. It enters wherever there is an opening and wreaks its havoc on all it can. All people can do to utilize fear and not be controlled by it is to live a life based on reality and faith…faith in the ultimate rightness of the universe and acceptance of our infinite anonymity in it.

Fear of the unknown can be one of the greatest fears. It envelops a gamut† of dysfunctions. It is probably the hardest fear to overcome or understand. Faith alone will not conquer it. A powerless life tends to perpetuate it. Only when a great enough level of pain is realized is there a chance to overcome it. When the pain of your reality exceeds your fear of the unknown, you will change†. Most change is driven by fear. Now that we have a basic understanding of fear, how do we determine its worth in our lives and utilize it to our benefit. Shall it drive us forward or back?

EDUCATION

(CHANGE)

GRACE: *an unmerited divine assistance given man for his regeneration or sanctification (to free from sin); mercy, pardon.*

—Unearned opportunity or favor.

Grace is a gift, it is not earned or deserved, it can only be received. Grace is not justice. It "is" mercy in its purest form. You cannot count on grace, you can only hope for it. Grace is an opportunity. If you work toward something and receive it, it is not a gift, you have earned it. If you have earned something you deserve to have it. You have received your just reward. The opportunity of the situation may have been grace, the accomplishment is "yours" for the actions you have taken. You do not get a paycheck by grace. Grace "may be" the reason you have a job.

If you need something you cannot achieve and it is made available to you, it is by grace that you have the possibility of acquiring it. Availability is not justice. Good or bad, justice comes from diligence† and deserving. Grace on the other hand, is not logical. It is mercy, more often than justice, which allows you the opportunity to achieve something you have not done anything to deserve. Much the same as we may freely give a homeless child attention and assistance without them doing anything to deserve it, grace allows us the opportunity to recreate our lives.

Grace, like faith, without works is nothing. Grace could be a welcome drink of water when you are thirsty. If you don't take the action available and drink, you are still thirsty. Grace allows good things to happen. Recognizing these things as grace usually comes after the fact. The cleaner your life is, the clearer grace becomes. Grace is kind, fate may be cruel and they are both random acts of the universe. Your response or lack thereof, when it is your turn, is uniquely yours.

Grace does not create change†, it only offers it. There is no event without action. Grace provides no opportunity without good intention. It does not lend itself to self-serving motivations, actions or accomplishment. It appears out of the universe often at times of desperation or pleading. It is not to be assumed or counted on, only hoped for. Without participation it is of no consequence. It does not pay rent or create serenity. It allows you to accomplish that which you cannot achieve by yourself. Like it or not, it's a God thing.

I came to recovery† broken and skeptical. I did not deserve a new life. I deserved to pay for the one I had created. I earned the opportunity to change my life by the acceptance and application of 12 Step principals. Grace opened those doors in front of me. "I" walked through them.

GOALS / PURPOSE

GOALS: *the ends toward which effort is directed.*

—Where you're headed.

PURPOSE: *a reason which something exists or is done, made, or used.*

—Why you're heading there.

Goals are intended destinations. They must be defined and envisioned, planned for and worked toward. Goals require effort to accomplish. Achieved, they give one confidence. Unrealized they can create an atmosphere of failure, low self-worth and loss of respect. Goals are reality. They determine direction and purpose of our lives. Their accomplishments are the booster rockets of our morale, their surrender, the weight we are destined to drag through life.

When I was a very young boy, I dreamed of being a scientist and discovering new things. I wanted to fly to the moon and taste the cheese. This was my first goal. Not supported, explained or defined, it was fantasized and assumed. I never forgot it or the shame associated with my first "B" grade. I was reminded of my failure at home. I was assured that I would never amount to anything, that I was not going to ever be anything but an orphan who owed his adoptees unfailing devotion since they chose to adopt him when no one else would. My goal should have been to get out of school with a diploma and continue to college. I accomplished that one without ever setting it. I had the intelligence to go anywhere in life but I had no purpose. I had given up any plan of doing anything productive in life. In hindsight, my only goal by the time I was seventeen, was to evade reality and responsibility at all costs. I felt shame because I had failed at my first goal and could not see the merits of what I "had" accomplished. I didn't set another goal or give purpose a serious thought until I was in my thirties.

Goals require direction. We do not just stumble upon them, they are plans. They must be realistic, achievable and available. We must believe in our goals in order to envision them. To envision our goals, we must understand them as well as our purpose. Our purpose supports their accomplishment. Unrealistic goals are fantasies. Goals without purpose are merely dreams.

To dream the impossible dream sounds good in song, but to see the obtainable goal is more realistic. Some people have lofty and numerous goals with strong purpose and devotion. Others just want out of the trailer park.

GRIEF

GRIEF: *deep and poignant (painfully affecting the feelings: piercing); distress caused by bereavement; a cause of such suffering.*

—An overwhelming and recurring distress, pain or memory that is in the past.

Let us begin with that which is commonly accepted without disputing its truth or relativity. Grief is a response (or reaction) to an event that has passed. Grief is real and often debilitating. It has no schedule. No one's level of grief is more or less important than another's. It is life altering and not pleasant. The accepted stages of grief are: 1) DENIAL, 2) ANGER, 3) BARGAINING, 4) DEPRESSION and 5) ACCEPTANCE. Mourning is the process of grieving. Bereavement is the actual losing of the person or thing.

That being said, I would like to focus on the journey through grief, not so much the resolution of it. The reasoning for this is that no two people resolve their grief issues the same. The motivation to resolve grief issues cannot be measured or predicted. My resolutions may not work for you and yours may not meet my needs. No level of understanding or acceptance can be determined to be required. Many people simply feel a sense of pain or loss and move on without further or future distress. This does not necessarily mean that they have a diminished sense of feeling. Perhaps rather, in their life, they have been taught or have come to accept loss as a part of life. It could be then that loss and its occurrence, although painful, is to be accepted as inevitable†. What is individually needed is the attainment of the destination to which we aspire, not a predetermined level of achievement to accomplish.

The accepted stages of grief have been determined by much study and research. Are these stages all that grief can be? Furthermore, are these stages limited only to grief, or are they an integral[†] part of a functional life. Can someone who has not experienced the debilitation that grief can bring, be ultimately qualified to write about it? If not, is their research less accurate? Accuracy is not at issue here, but further depth or definition could be required. These phases of grief are hardly an archetype[†] of resolution.

Timeless sympathy, rather than solution directed motivation, can further the necessary damage and alteration brought about by grief. Grief recovery[†] and resolution can only be measured at its completion, not by its depth or duration. As a paradigm[†], the five stages of grief lack full disclosure. This paradigm paralysis prevents shift from taking place. To disagree or dispute requires either more or opposing information[†] lest it be denial in its purest form.

Grief is painful and "life ain't always fair".

GENETICS

GENETICS: a branch of biology that deals with the heredity and variation of organisms; the genetic makeup and phenomena of an organism, type, group or condition.

—**"Who" you're made from.**

Scientifically, genetics is about the origin of species, their development and current state. Psychological genetics is about what comprised the person you came to be, from before you had a choice in the matter, through the events that preceded today. These are the things that comprise who and what you are currently. If we can recreate the map of our origins through the journey we have taken to get to today, we have an account of whom, why and how we are.

Genetics is a science of mapping. A map from 1979 isn't much use in today's world if you need in depth information[†]. Things have changed considerably in the past years. Some things are basically unchanged but progress has changed the landscape of what was. Growth has left its mark, or scar, as the case may be. Old roads have become freeways and farmland, subdivisions. Neighborhoods are gone for the sake of progress. The point is, whether we accept it or not, "things" have changed. Genetics is the original landscape of our life. Time and experience have altered our lives to the point that our origins are often unrecognizable. We've abandoned what "was," for what we've created. This is not about blame, not good or bad, it's simply our current reality, our up to date life map.

How a person is raised has a profound[†] effect on their view of reality. It does not alter reality, only that person's perspective[†] of it. This socio-genetics is more about "how" than "whom," however it is necessary to understand all the aspects of genetics in order to alter their natural course. The socio[†] aspects of genetics are more open to alteration than the physiological. Our historical disposition[†] to act in a certain manner is adjustable. A person may learn new information[†] that can change their reality. They cannot change their blood type or their susceptibility[†] to certain diseases[†]. If a person is not satisfied with their life's course, new information allows the opportunity to redirect it. The information will not change your nationality, parents, point of origin or past. It may however, allow you to enjoy the future in ways never considered.

Our skeletal[†] make-up, hair and eye color, and skin color are genetically determined by our birth parents and their parents before them. We have no control over those facts, they just "are." Our pre-disposition for certain diseases is beyond our control. Knowledge of our history gives us an insight into what to expect. New knowledge prevents us from repeating past mistakes.

HABITS

HABIT: *manner of conducting oneself; a behavior pattern acquired by frequent repetition; an acquired mode of behavior that has become nearly or completely involuntary; addiction.*

—Something you do repeatedly without forethought[†].

The founder of the Public School System in this country, Horace Mann, once said, "Habit is like a cable. We weave a thread of it every day, and at last we can't break it." Good or bad, habits can have a great deal of strength in our lives. Habits don't just happen, they are developed. Generally they are easier to develop than to overcome. They serve us until we serve them. Addiction is a habit, a very bad one. We have a say in our habits. We participate in them. People can be empowered to understand the influence habits may have on their life, and to overcome those that affect them negatively.

Habits may be a powerful influence in life; they can be supportive or destructive. Healthy habits stabilize life and promote virtues such as health, responsibility and progress. Unhealthy or negative habits can deter us from the benefits and joys of life. Repetition is a requirement of any habit, whatever it may be. In order for an action to become habitual, one must do it repeatedly. Some habits are subtle to the person doing them; some are only recognizable when brought to that person's attention. Some actions are more habitual than others in that they gain strength very quickly. Certain drugs most certainly fit into this category. Picking your nose habitually does not develop as quickly, or become as unmanageable, as smoking crack cocaine.

Habits can be developed inadvertently from unconscious

repetition, or deliberately, with a great deal of determination and sacrifice. A habit is not the result of a single act, but rather the recurrence of past actions. Habits are by their very nature actions...actions that are being repeated. The habit of brushing your teeth immediately when you wake up is not bad. If you brush until your gums bleed, you are probably overdoing it. Overdoing a habit is obsessive at least, addictive at worst. Addiction is the ultimate bad habit. It is the hardest to amend and most destructive of all. Addiction is all encompassing in its evil. It ruins lives, families, organizations and relationships. Its toxic tentacles weave their way to the depths of the soul where they feed on the very essence† of life leaving only shame and degradation to the participant. Bleak, huh?

If habit is in fact a cable, and we do in fact weave a thread of it every day, how do we break it? A cable is a multi-strand material. A chain is only as strong as its weakest link, but a cable is as strong as the sum total of all the individual strands combined. We become empowered to break it only after acknowledging this fact and begin to sever one strand at a time, one day at a time, until we can destroy that final first strand.

PEER PRESSURE

PEER: *One that is of equal standard with another.*

PRESSURE: *The burden of physical or mental distress.*

—Desire to be accepted and/or feeling of influence by others.

Have you ever been accused of doing this or that because of peer pressure?" How did you feel at the time? Attacked? Guilty? Ashamed? Why is it when some person or group attacks our friends, we feel the need to defend them? Do we feel a sense of duty to stand up for them even when we believe them to be wrong? This may be one of the simplest forms of peer-pressure.

Peer pressure is not necessarily a negative influence. If the people you choose to associate with are intent on getting good grades, you have peer pressure to achieve that goal also. Peer pressure is not mandatory[†], it's a choice[†]. You are responsible for the amount of influence you allow others to have on your life. "Just Say No" doesn't always cut it. "Just Say Something - And Stand For It!" means "more" This implies[†] that you know what you're saying. It also makes you responsible for having the knowledge of the implications[†] of your statement. This may take some effort and serious thought! You may need to search out information[†] from other sources. You may indeed have to even search for those other sources. You can only become a better person for doing it. It may also give you a better understanding of who you are and the type of world you have chosen to live in.

The laws of physics have many similarities to peer pressure. One of those laws state, "Water seeks its own level." This is also true in your choice† of peers. You seek your social level in your peers. Seeking is a choice. You make it. If you are not satisfied with your level, you alone must find the inner courage to abandon it and strive for another. Until you change your own social standards, you cannot move from this peer influence. Another law states, "Electricity follows the path of least resistance". Peer pressure is like that too. It is easier to rationalize why we should stay in a situation than summoning the courage to change or leave it. Resistance to change is normal. What is familiar can be expected, even if it is not pleasurable. Who is to say that the unknown could not be even more painful?

Misery loves company, so our peers often urge us to remain in bad situations so they will not be alone. Knowing we need to change and putting it off is not healthy. Tomorrow may be too late. If we are coasting, we're probably going downhill. The opportunity to effect meaningful change is momentary at best. Fear is usually why people delay change but pain can be a great motivator. When the pain of our reality exceeds our fear of the unknown, we will change. It is always easier to lower your standards than to stand for them. Character is built on overcoming resistance. If we put as much energy into developing ourselves as we do in rationalizing behaviors, we would be much happier.

This "peer balance," is never constant. As we change, so do our peers. Today's followers may be tomorrow's leaders. Position is never constant. There are too many people jostling for position. Some people strive to be leaders. Some allow themselves to be stepping-stones to more ruthless achievers. Even the most ruthless of people would rather walk on smooth stones than sharp rocks. Knowledge can define you as a person as well as shape you into a rock not easy to tread upon. Followers always need a leader. By their very nature, followers are vulnerable to the whims of those who lead them. They are like leaves in a stream, drifting to the rhythm of the strongest current. Content to be led, resolved to fate, and another's direction, they blindly follow without resistance. They assume this to be some sort of destined journey to the sea on one of life's lesser streams. It appears so worthwhile and almost honorable. Only at the sewer's mouth do they realize their folly. Their leaders are exposed. They are just the mud surrounding us in life's great final cesspool, slowly sinking into the silt. Ugly vision? Maybe I went too far—maybe not.

RESPONSIBILITY

RESPONSIBILITY: *the quality or state of being accountable: reliability, trustworthiness; something for which one is responsible; burden.*

—Owning yourself or being. Standing for what you believe.

Have you ever been called irresponsible? I have, and I "have" been. There have been times in my life that I have been called irresponsible when in fact I was doing my very best to accomplish something. Some of these times I was acting without adequate knowledge and sometimes what I was trying so hard to accomplish was in itself irresponsible. What about those times when I was wrongly accused of not being responsible? The easiest way for most people to shift responsibility is to give it to someone else. This manipulation† is widespread in our society†, from the leaders of government passing the buck down the ladder, to the homeless who sit idly blaming the rest of society for their misfortune. Life will never be entirely fair and no one will ever be totally blameless. I believe the best we can ever hope for is that we as individuals "own" our part in life. This of course would assume that we have at least a general knowledge of whom and what we are as individuals.

Some say responsibility is the ability to respond. I believe they have left out a critical word, that being "functionally." Everyone is capable of responding. Everyone's responses are not necessarily functional. Reactions are responses without responsibility. It takes conscience effort to "own" your response and know what it entails.

Life is a constant state of change. Circumstances are hardly ever duplicated. If I find myself in duplicating circumstance, it is rarely something healthy. Either I have failed to grow from the past or I have not acknowledged life's inevitable[†] and constant change. Change is a requirement of growth, and growth is responsible living.

TYPES OF RESPONSIBILITY

PERSONAL: *accountability*   _____

PHYSICAL: *hygiene*   _____

CIVIC: *obeying the law*   _____

FINANCIAL: *paying the bills*   _____

MORAL: *doing right things*   _____

FAMILIAL: *doing your part*   _____

PARENTAL: *leading by example*   _____

OTHER: _____

SPONSORSHIP

(SHARING)

DISCIPLINE

DISCIPLINE: punishment; instruction (obsolete); control gained by enforcing obedience or order; orderly or prescribed conduct or pattern of behavior; self-control; a rule or system of rules governing conduct or activity.

—Supervision required to maintain order.

SELF-DISCIPLINE: correction or regulation of oneself for the sake of improvement.

—Voluntary compliance to one's own beliefs that maintains their direction in life.

By its very nature discipline is not pleasant, it is oppressive. Who enjoys forced compliance to other's rules or demands? Why then do people constantly put themselves in situations where it becomes necessary? Have we as a society[†] become so self-centered as to require force to maintain order? Is our self-control dependent on responsibility to others? Do we not have basic values that direct our actions? Is self-discipline so difficult that personal responsibility has no influence? Discipline is only required when a problem or dilemma exists.

Children require discipline to mature. Nurturing[†] is necessary to balance this discipline. Without both, discipline becomes tyranny[†]. Tyranny promotes anarchy[†]. Anarchy destroys order. Without order there is chaos. Society cannot exist with chaos. Oppressive laws are required to maintain discipline. Sound familiar?

Discipline is not instinctive[†], it must be learned. Ideally, it is a by-product of nurturing. Nurturing provides a person with an atmosphere of learning as well as a sense of self and value.

Without nurturing[†], discipline must be imposed. Even with proper nurturing, discipline must sometimes be forced. If a person will not exercise self-control to act acceptably they may be disciplined. This discipline is meant to alter unacceptable behavior so that it does not reoccur. The dispenser of discipline is not meant to enjoy it, neither is the receiver. By its nature, discipline is not supposed to be fun.

In today's society we have an unbearable number of young people who live their lives in contempt of discipline. Is this a product of our society, or were they reared in households that did not instill a basic concept of discipline? If you do not have knowledge of something, how can you teach it? The family structure in America today is at a crossroads. We are on the verge of abandoning what those who came before us created. My question is, "If our forefathers lived in today's world, what would they have created?" We as a society need to take action to learn what we have missed. Until we understand that our lives can be productive and peaceful if we work toward that, we will and must be subjected to discipline from others.

USE - ABUSE - DEPENDENCE - ADDICTION

What's the difference? To some there is none. If you use any mind altering chemical you must be a drug addict or alcoholic. To others there is no such thing as dependence, only weak willed people with a moral deficiency. And there are the chosen few who believe that what they ingest is their business and that they can stop whenever they please. Some are even right in this assumption! The majority of users will never suffer any ill effects from their use. This book is for them too, because you can never foresee the need for the information[†] presented herein.

In our culture it seems that the use of mind-altering chemicals is perpetuated by advertising campaigns as well as many medical professionals. With little or no consideration for the long-term effects of this use, we continue to bombard our people with the glamour of drinking and smoking. Wide mouth beer cans are the latest rage. "Ice" beverages seem so cool? Our billboards are full of advertising directly aimed at drinking. Sex sells, especially to the young and impressionable. I haven't seen "Middle Age Executives Gone Wild" advertised. It's all about sex, drugs, alcohol and youth. Viagra is the new drug of choice. The price is yet to be paid, the bill still hasn't been sent.

Medical science has developed so called cures for depression as well as other psychological problems with this or that pill. This is not to say that medications of this type are not sometimes in order. They allow patients a calm level playing field to address their problems. This is the time for introspect. Now is the opportunity for change. Less emphasis should be put on the effects of the medication and more responsibility should be put on the patient to treat the symptoms that prompted the prescription. Perhaps doctors should be required to ask what the patient plans to do about the problem after the symptoms subside, before they ask what insurance coverage they have? Is the patient or doctor responsible?

This concept of responsibility appears out of place today. If you're sick, how can you be responsible for your illness? Shouldn't someone be liable? Attorneys will litigate this till the end of time. I hope not with me! I choose to believe that if I am not healthy, I must find the root of my discomfort, not a chemical to make me feel differently. In some cases mood altering chemicals are able to alleviate the symptoms of our discomfort but the patient must assume responsibility for change or run the risk of becoming dependent on their medication to function in a normal fashion. Used appropriately I believe modern chemical treatment to be a Godsend, irresponsible prescribing to be abuse.

Abuse of mind-altering substances does not make a person dependent. It is the first step to becoming that way though! Over a period of time a person reaches a point where nothing seems tolerable straight. You learn to function on the edges of reality. Function becomes existing----- which becomes surviving-----hopefully. The longer you survive, the greater the chances of dying become. You stop when you become willing enough----- not when you find a new drug.

USE
— *Willful ingestion of a substance for purely social or medical reasons.*

Anyone who uses any mood altering substance is capable of becoming a substance abuser. If you never use a mood-altering chemical, you can never abuse one! If a person is prescribed a painkiller for a toothache and takes as needed according to the doctor's advice, they should never feel the mood altering capabilities of their medication. It should relieve their pain without any side-effects. If they take it long enough, they may develop a tolerance to the medication and suffer withdrawal symptoms when they stop. This type of issue is easily dealt with on its own, but usually is compounded by other symptoms or problems. A normal drinker may imbibe at times and never become dependent. Marijuana use does not fit in this category since almost all use is intended to alter perception and mood. I have yet to meet anyone who uses pot without intending to become high. This brings us to the next topic.

ABUSE
—Deliberate over use of a substance to achieve an altered reality.

If you use a mood altering substance with the intent of altering your reality, you are abusing the substance. Going out with the intention of getting drunk is alcohol abuse. Anytime anyone ingests a mood altering chemical with the intent of altering reality is abuse. Medically prescribed drugs that alter brain chemistry can be easily abused. Taken properly they balance brain chemistry. This is not abuse. Abuse is taking more than the prescribed amount with the intent to feel high. If a person gets drunk or high, it is more intent or irresponsibility than an accident. The excuse, "I just had a little too much" is not acceptable to a responsible person. Whatever the consequences of that behavior are, they belong to the individual who had "too much," not to society†. If a social drinker becomes drunk, that person is abusing alcohol. Pot smokers are usually in the process of abusing marijuana. Abuse of chemicals is not the beginning of a problem, use is. If you do not use chemicals, you cannot abuse them. If you never abuse chemicals you certainly can never become dependent on them.

DEPENDENCE
—Needing to be under the influence of a substance to enjoy life.

When mood altering chemicals are abused in such great amounts or over a long enough time periods, the phenomenon of dependency occurs. At this point it is as if a person crosses an invisible line into dis-function, desperation and denial. This is the point of no return for most people. At this time the wheels of care-free partying fall off. No one ever gets to this point by accident. No one ever found a way back across the imaginary invisible line to normal abuse. Normal has become non-existent; it will never be enough again. A person "MUST" accept responsibility for their predicament. It cannot be someone else's fault. Simply put, "You've shot up all your ammunition, better get the hell outta the war." There is nothing easy about facing or accepting this responsibility. The bridges you have crossed have all burnt, there's no way back. Forward is not a bad option at this time. In reality, forward is all that is left short of dis-function, desperation and denial. It was once written, "Wish I didn't know now, what I didn't know then". Truer words could not have been written for the dependent person. The fact must be realized by the afflicted person that the rules as well as the boundaries have changed, permanently. If you never used mood altering chemicals, you could have never abused them. Had you not abused them, you could have never become dependent. The only thing worse than dependency, is addiction.

ADDICTION
—Needing a substance to exist or function.

Addiction is when you, as a person, cannot function in a normal manner without being under the influence of a mood altering chemical. Life is unbearable until you achieve an altered state. In this lifestyle, the chemical becomes the reason for living. Without it, you are unable to accomplish the most minor tasks. With it, they lose their importance. At this point of existence nothing means more to the addict than their chemical. It takes precedence over friends, family, jobs and relationships. The addict has no moral strength to fall back on, no self esteem or confidence to protect themselves with and no hope of change. This seemingly hopeless state can not be recovered from alone. Professionals generally agree that the most effective treatment available is from others who have somehow recovered from addiction. No one has ever, to my knowledge, aspired to reach this level of despair and hopelessness. No one has ever risen one morning and said, "I think I'll become an addict today". Every person who has ever been an addict has laid down countless nights and said, "This has to end, I'm quitting tomorrow." You cannot quit being an addict. You can quit being addicted, but you will always be one relapse from your old addictions.

FREEDOM

FREEDOM: the quality or state of being free as, the absence of necessity, coercion, or constraint in choice or action.

—No shoes, no home, no problem—or, "NO RESPONSIBILITY."

"Freedom's just another word for nothing left to lose" is a phrase that speaks volumes about the decade of the sixties in America. I was there, although most memories are foggy. The wanderlust and inquisitive notion of the day sent many people across the globe looking for real freedom. The missing ingredient was responsibility. Freedom was fun until the bill came. Life is not carefree, and freedom is not free at all. A price must be paid for anything of value. The price of freedom can be high, and worth every cost paid.

By definition, freedom without responsibility is chaos. Without constraint to govern our actions, there can be no order. Without order there can be no responsibility, and without responsibility there can be no growth. Without growth we stagnate and die. Freedom does not alleviate us of our commitments, but rather opens life up to the possibilities we face. Therein lays the dilemma. Freedom allows us change, but requires us to accept responsibility for it.

In this country we enjoy freedom to the extent never known in history. We are not required to conform to any ideology or set of boundaries. We are innocent until "proven" guilty. We have the right to an education†, free movement, and choice† in personal matters. This may sound idealistic or liberal, but every citizen of this country has certain freedoms. All that is required of them is to obey a few rules. These rules were not designed to be overbearing, although many may have become such, but rather to promote these freedoms we enjoy. Unless a person is willing to pack-up and move to another country, they must honor the rules that govern this one. America is a long way from perfect, but on the planet today it's as good as it gets when you talk about freedom.

Universally we all have the freedom to exist. If not, we wouldn't. This concept is simple in its truth, yet complex in its implications.[†] As Gabran said in "The Madman" even a thief in jail is free from another thief. You would have to read the whole thing to understand. If we exist, we are. If we're free, we are free. The strongest prisons have no bars or doors. Prison for many people is fear. Freedom is scary and sometimes not participating is safer. As with all things, there is a price to pay. To participate fully in freedom one must accept personal responsibility. If your belief is that someone already paid for your freedom, you still must accept the responsibilities of it.

Historically, lack of freedom has caused more wars than hate has. War is a struggle for power more than a struggle for freedom. Freedom takes the blame for many self-centered agendas. It leaves us confused and burdened when we look deeply into its ramifications. With all the ambiguity, freedom is still the best game in town

OPINION / FACT

OPINION: *a view, judgment, or appraisal formed in the mind about a particular matter; belief stronger than impression and less strong than positive knowledge.*

—What you think, say or believe.

FACT: *a thing done; the quality of being actual.*

—What you know to be true, what can be substantiated.

I can factually relate to another person, my experiences. They remain opinions to that person until they have personally experienced them. This concept is a double-edged sword, for if we represent things as facts, and expect another person to assume them as true, we must be able to substantiate† them by word and deed in our own lives. On the other hand, if we believe what another says without a basis of trust in that person we are fools to say the least. Opinions are better communicated as suggestions, not truths. Many an honest person ended up a liar by stating opinions as fact.

Facts are based in truth or personal history. When I was a child I was told the stove was hot. Upon further study I came to believe that as a fact. There is a natural flow to "that" information†, investigation and conviction. When I was young I was told that I would never be able to repay my parents for adopting me. I tried, I failed, I quit. It was my opinion that they could not be repaid. Had I exhausted my options to repay them and not been successful, it may have become factual. The fact became my unwillingness to continue to try, not their unwillingness to be repaid for my adoption. Facts are unyielding, unemotional, and indifferent. They are not rationalized, only accepted. We can only hope to discover them and understand their effects on our lives.

Opinions are like excuses, "Everybody's had one." That's not to say there is no merit to opinions. Opinions are valuable tools in learning. Opinions may open the door of speculation; urge investigation and implementation[†] without making any demands on the recipient. Opinions are sharing information[†] with another person. If they have use for the opinion, it is free to them. If they don't, it's free to leave.

If I were to state a fact, and expect you to believe it, I would be making an assumption. That assumption would be that what I had related to you would; 1) be understood, 2) be believed, 3) have value, 4) achieve the same results in your life as in mine. That's quite an assumption. Whose fault would it be if you failed based on my facts? Was your failure due to my methods or your madness? Are you destined to relive my experiences? Am I so intelligent that I know who you are, how you feel, what you know? Am I so egotistical that I believe my way is the only way for you to understand life? Are you so gullible that you take what I say as fact without scrutiny?

This comparison is not so much a learning venue[†] as a life venue. Facts are demands, opinions are options. Facts are not created; they are discovered. There's no credit in opinions; or reward from facts. Facts are apparent; opinions must be considered, investigated and implemented[†] before they may become facts. It's all in the presentation. Most people would rather take suggestions than orders.

REHABILITATION: *to restore or bring to a condition of health or useful and constructive activity.*

—AN ACTION.
—Abstaining from further damage by chemical abuse.
—Not using chemicals after knowledge of harmful effects.
—Becoming physically well by abstaining from chemicals.

RECOVERY: *the act, process, or an instance of recovering;*
Recovering: to find or identify again; to save from loss and restore to usefulness

—A PROCESS.
—Changing, emotional growth, developing a new life type or style.

I regularly hear the statement, "I went to rehab and it didn't do any good." "Don't blame the rehab," is my pat response. "Were you physically healthier when you left than when you arrived? Were you able to think clearer the day you got out than the day you went in? Did you learn anything about yourself, life or chemicals while you were there?" The answer is usually "Yes" to the above. The mission of a rehab is well defined above. Entering into a rehab setting is an action. Some people are dragged, kicking and screaming; some go quietly. It does not matter how a person arrives as long as they leave with more information† than they came with. There are all kinds of rehabs. The common denominator they all share is an attempt to restore their clients to a more healthy condition. They do this with structure, diet and education†. The goal of rehab is to allow a person to make more rational, informed decisions about their future.

Rehabs are not usually detoxification centers although some have detox wards. Detox simply stabilizes a person medically. The effects of heavy or long term chemical abuse can cause serious health issues. It would not be safe for some "rehab" clients to immediately go "Cold Turkey" (immediate withdrawal) from drugs. They are not in good enough physical and / or mental health to enter a rehabilitation center. Detox centers serve as an important link in the cycle of recovery†. It's highly recommended that rehab follows detox immediately. Detox centers often act as referral agencies for their clients, assisting them in finding appropriate facilities. After rehab transitional living environments are available to assist people in their re-entry to normal (hopefully) lifestyles.

A main theme of both detox and rehab is informing a person that there is in fact a future available to them, that they are not unique or alone, that others have recovered from this seemingly hopeless state and gone on to lead very productive happy lives. The most common way this is accomplished is through a recovery network or program.

Recovery is more than a group you join or a meeting you attend. Those are actions. Recovery is a dedication to growth. It is a desire to live happy and free. Recovery is about function in a dysfunctional world. It is a process that's speed is in direct relation to the commitment you make to it.

SEXUALITY

SEXUALITY: *the quality or state of being sexual; the condition of having sex; sexual activity; expression of sexual receptivity or interest, especially when excessive.*

—What you do, with who, and why.

Sex has been around for a long time. Since the beginning it has been used to show affection, share emotion and create children. The dark side of sex is manipulation[†] and domination, or control of others. Sounded great until the end, right? Sexual problems usually lie in the end of that last statement. If no one is being hurt, all must be well, right? Not necessarily so. Today's world is full of sex and sexual innuendos[†]. The permissiveness of society[†] has taken all of the mystery and much of the allure[†] away from sexuality and left it a cold and often manipulative act. Addicts and alcoholics are easily swept into the eddy of sexual gratification without worth or responsibility.

Consensual sexuality may best be defined as giving a piece of your soul away. Would you do this without receiving anything in return? What would you have returned? The healthy response would be, "A part of another's soul." Too often in today's sexuality, the trade out is an exchange of dysfunction instead of souls. You fix me and I'll fix you is not functional sexuality. If individual worth is based on attraction from a sexual partner, it does not bring much depth to the relationship. Something is better than nothing may be more destructive to this type of interaction than not having it. Self-seeking and self-respect should be determining factors in any sexual relationship.

How does one determine the health or function of a sexual encounter? The first question would have to be, "Is this a secret?" Secrets are not healthy in relationships, and a sexual encounter is a relationship. If something is a secret, why would one share it? Simply put, a secret's power is diminished when shared. Shared is not promoted or repeated though. Exposing your own secrets is the beginning of healing. If a sexual act is shameful or a secret for any reason, steps must be taken to resolve the issue, not secretly perpetuate it. Sexuality is one of the most gratifying experiences one can have in context and honesty. Without common ground and truth it becomes twisted and dark. In this state it perpetuates dysfunction, shame and guilt. No good can come of it, after the "lovin."

Sex sells! A zillionaire came up with that thought. Ever since man has tried to get the attention of his fellows, sexuality has been an attraction. Sexuality is used to sell things that aren't remotely sexual, distract people from the truth in matters and products, and to lure impressionable people into the world of fame and fortune where they can only contribute to the perpetration. Sexuality does not equal brains, nor do brains equate to sexual attraction to all people. A "brainiac" may be the sensual dream of one person whereas another cares little, if at all, about intelligence. What is presented must be truthful and achievable in order to be functional. Truth is in the presentation, function is in the person.

What do you bring to the table with your sexuality? How whole are you? Do you give more than you seem to receive, or take whatever is offered? Is there a balance in your sexuality? Nothing is more swaying to a person than sexuality. It covers up a myriad† of sins and inadequacies, gives outlet to frustration and loneliness, and always costs something. It can heal a relationship, but never a person. It does not fix anything. Healthy sexuality is sharing† openly and honestly. Without these parameters† it is abuse or manipulation†. Within a commitment it can be a spring morning after a rain, together, quiet.

When is sex an addiction? It's obvious why it "could" be. If sexuality is used as a tool or weapon, if it fixes or eases one's desires without fulfillment, it can easily become an addiction. Addictions by their very nature change the way we feel. Sexuality is all about feelings. When undesirable feelings are altered with sexuality, they no longer have real validity. The sexual act changes their reality. What was felt prior to the act is masked by the intensity of the act itself. Recurrence of sexuality to avoid negative or painful feelings only works for a time. Eventually, the real basis of one's feelings emerges and must be addressed without the smokescreen, or distraction of sexuality.

Sexuality is not passion, but passion may be an integral[†] part of sexuality. Passion is an intensity of feeling. Without passion, sexuality leans toward self centered manipulation[†] or abuse. In a passionate, committed relationship, passion is an attribute[†], not a deterrent. For fun and for free does not imply commitment, therefore any associated passion could be better defined as lust. Lust is intense but not passionate. Lust is also detrimental to healthy boundaries.

Sexuality is part of who we are and how we act. We cannot be whole without acknowledging our personal sexuality. How it's used or abused has a profound[†] effect on how well we live and to some extent, how long. It can be an important part of our lives without having undue power or persuasion over our decisions. Sex is not a weapon, tool or an object to barter with. Sexuality can be an angel of mercy or the antichrist, depending on its use and intention. Know this, "The world is full of kings and queens, who'll blind your eyes and steal your dreams."

RELATIVITY

RELATIVITY: the quality or state of being relative; the quality of being dependent for existence, or determined in nature, value or quality, by relation to something else.

RELATIVE: a thing having relation to, or connection with, or necessary dependence on, another thing.

—What comes around, goes around.

Did anyone ever say to you, "It's all relative?" How about, "I can't relate." Have you ever felt disconnected from life? Perhaps you were, it was relative. Relativity is reality. It cannot be out of balance, it is balance. Relativity is always dependent on something, it's comparative and progressive. Relativity is the natural order of things. Relativity is non-judgmental and has no power to change; it changes when you do. Relativity is circumstantial, time sensitive, and situational.

The essence† of relativity is comparison. It is a matter of cause and effect. For every action, there is an opposite and equal reaction. Everything you do, say, feel or plan, has an effect. Consider this, somewhere, somehow, out in the universe, everything is connected. Some of it has not happened yet, but given certain variables, it may. "Your" relativity is based on "your" reality. Relativity is "your" reality. Ideally, you get what you give. If life were a target, reality would be the bulls-eye. Everything else is dependant on its relativity to the bulls-eye.

Behaviors are relative to feelings. Yesterdays feelings are not necessarily relevant† today. New behaviors are relative to new feelings. There is little incentive to change functional behavior; it usually results in positive responses. If yesterday was not functional or pleasant, new behaviors might be appropriate today. The new behaviors would be relative to the anticipated outcome of them. This is circumstantial or time sensitive relativity, wherein at another time what matters now, would not, and vice versa.

Everything has a natural balance. There is a connection between how you act and how you feel. If one is altered, it becomes out of balance with the other, and one or the other must adjust. The adjustment or change then becomes relevant[†] to, or in other words, connected to, the new behavior. Relativity is alterable by action. If you go into a rowdy skid row bar, would you expect to see the same behavior as you see in an upscale dinner club? Would the customers dress the same, order from a similar menu? This is situational relativity,

Relativity is not what is, it is why it matters. It's not necessarily truth, but perception. What I see as relative, may have absolutely no meaning to you. Who's right? Who cares, if neither one of us has an effect on the others life. Relativity is more of an explanation than a reason, it cannot justify, only identify. I can share my life, my love, my reality; not my relativity.

BIBLIOGRAPHY

I've not been able to locate the proper verbiage to say that if you believe that you said it first, go ahead and take credit for it. I don't believe in new facts, only new ways of explaining what is and has become. The fact is, there was a beginning and there'll probably be an end. We exist in the middle somewhere, only for a time. What we do in the time we have is up to us. True leadership, we find, depends upon able example and not upon vain displays of power or glory.

Big Book of Alcoholics Anonymous (1st, 2nd and 3rd additions)

Twelve Steps and Twelve Traditions of Alcoholics Anonymous

Various 12 Step approved publications

Many 12 Step un-approved publications

Innumerable 12 step meetings since May 5, 1982

All Recovery Programs and their participants

This page reserved for the names of all who claim responsibility for, or authorship of, any part or content of this publication.

_____

_____

_____

_____

_____

_____

_____

_____

_____

_____

_____

_____

_____

_____

_____

_____

_____

_____

GLOSSARY

This list is comprised of words, in this book, whose meanings have been questioned or misunderstood. Word usage is always relevant in communication. Many words have a multitude of meanings depending on the context in which they are used. For this reason the complete definitions of the following words has been reduced to the tense and or usage that applies to this text.

Action: *an act of will; a thing done: deed; the accomplishment of a thing usually over a period of time, in stages, or with the possibility of repetition.*

Admission: *acknowledgment that a fact or statement is true.*

Allude: *to make indirect reference comments alluding to an earlier discussion.*

Allure: *power of attraction or fascination: charm.*

Anarchy: *absence or denial of any authority or established order.*

Anecdote: *a usually short narrative of an interesting, amusing, or biographical incident.*

Apathy: *lack of feeling or emotion: impassiveness; lack of interest or concern; indifference.*

Aplomb: *complete and confident composure or self-assurance: poise.*

Arbitrate: *decide, determine.*

Archetype: *the original pattern or model of which all things of the same type are representations or copies: prototype; also : a perfect example.*

Assimilation: *the process of receiving new facts or of responding to new situations in conformity with what is already available to consciousness.*

Attribute: *an inherent characteristic; an object closely associated with or belonging to a specific person.*

Benevolent: *marked by or disposed to doing good (a benevolent donor); organized for the purpose of doing good (a benevolent society); marked by or suggestive of goodwill (benevolent smiles).*

Bolster: *a structural part designed to eliminate friction or provide support or bearing.*

Change: *to make different in some particular; to make radically different: transform (can't change human nature).*

Chaos: *a state of utter confusion.*

Choice: *the act of choosing; selection: power of choosing; option.*

Chronic: *marked by long duration or frequent recurrence.*

Clarification: *to free of confusion; to make understandable.*

Cohesion: *the act or state of sticking together tightly.*

Conducive: *tending to promote or assist.*

Credence: *mental acceptance as true or real (give credence to gossip); credibility, belief.*

Crucial: *important or essential as resolving a crisis: decisive; marked by final determination of a doubtful issue (the ~ game of a series).*

Cyclic: *of, relating to, or being a cycle b: moving in cycles (cyclic time).*

Deduce: *to determine by deduction; to trace the course of.*

Delegation: *the act of empowering to act for another; a group of persons chosen to represent others.*

Diffidence: *hesitant in acting or speaking through lack of self-confidence; archaic: distrustful; reserved, unassertive.*

Diligence: *the attention and care legally expected or required of a person (as a party to a contract).*

Dire: *desperately urgent (dire need); extreme.*

Discovery: *to make known or visible; expose: display; to obtain sight or knowledge of for the first time: find (discover the solution); find out (discovered he was out of gas).*

Disease: *a condition that impairs normal function.*

Disposition: *prevailing tendency, mood, or inclination; temperamental makeup; the tendency of something to act in a certain manner under given circumstances.*

Ecclesiastical: *suitable for use in a church.*

Education: *the action or process of educating or of being educated; also: a stage of such a process; the knowledge and development resulting from an educational process.*

Emote: *to give expression to emotion especially in acting.*

Epitome: *a typical or ideal example.*

Essence: *the permanent as contrasted with the accidental element of being; the individual, real, or ultimate nature of a thing especially as opposed to its existence (a painting that captures the essence of the land); the properties or attributes† by means of which something can be placed in its proper class or identified as being what it is.*

Extolling: *to praise highly: glorify.*

Forethought: *a thinking or planning out in advance: premeditation; consideration for the future.*

Futility: *the quality or state of being futile: uselessness; a useless act or gesture.*

Gamut: *an entire range or series.*

Germination: *to come into being: evolve: to cause to sprout or develop.*

Glean: *to gather bit by bit, to pick over in search of relevant material; find out.*

Implement: *carry out, accomplish; especially: to give practical effect to and ensure of actual fulfillment by concrete measures.*

Implementation: *carry out, accomplish; especially: to give practical effect to and ensure of actual fulfillment by concrete measures; to provide instruments or means of expression for.*

Implementing: *carry out, accomplish: to give practical effect to and ensure of actual fulfillment by concrete measures.*

Implications: *something implied: a possible significance.*

Implies: *to contain potentially; to express indirectly.*

Incongruent: *discordant, incompatible, not agreeing.*

Inconsequential: *illogical; irrelevant; of no significance: unimportant.*

Indignation: *anger aroused by something unjust, unworthy, or mean.*

Indolence: *inclination to laziness: sloth.*

Inevitable: *incapable of being avoided or evaded (an inevitable outcome).*

Influential: *the act or power of producing an effect without apparent exertion of force or direct exercise of command.*

Information: *the communication or reception of knowledge or intelligence; knowledge obtained from investigation, study, or instruction.*

Inhibition: *the act of inhibiting : the state of being inhibited; something that forbids, debars, or restricts; an inner impediment to free activity, expression, or functioning; a mental process imposing restraint upon behavior or another mental process (as a desire).*

Innuendos: *an oblique allusion: hint, insinuation; especially: a veiled or equivocal reflection on character or reputation; the use of such allusions.*

Insolence: *insultingly contemptuous in speech or conduct: overbearing.*

Instinctive: *prompted by natural instinct: arising spontaneously.*

Integral: *essential to completeness.*

Integration: *coordination of mental processes into a normal effective personality or with the individual's environment.*

Intrinsically: *belonging to the essential nature or constitution of a thing (the intrinsic worth of a gem) (the intrinsic brightness of a star).*

Inventory: *a list of traits, preferences, attitudes, interests, or abilities used to evaluate personal characteristics or skills.*

Mandatory: *containing or constituting a command: obligatory.*

Manipulation: *to manage or utilize skillfully; to control or play upon by artful, unfair, or insidious means especially to one's own advantage; to change by artful or unfair means so as to serve one's purpose.*

Myriad: *a great number.*

Mystical: *having a spiritual meaning or reality that is neither apparent to the senses nor obvious to the intelligence; involving or having the nature of an individual's direct subjective communion with God or ultimate reality.*

Narcissistic: *egotism; love of one's own body.*

Negate: *deny the existence or truth of; to cause to be ineffective or invalid.*

Nurturing: *educate; to further the development of.*

Paradigm: *a philosophical and theoretical framework of a scientific school or discipline within which theories, laws, and generalizations and the experiments performed in support of them are formulated; broadly: a philosophical or theoretical framework of any kind.*

Paradox: *a statement that is seemingly contradictory or opposed to common sense and yet is perhaps true.*

Parameters: *limit, boundary usually used in plural.*

Perspective: *point of view; the capacity to view things in their true relations or relative importance.*

Precarious: *depending on the will or pleasure of another; dependent on uncertain premises: dubious; dependent on chance circumstances, unknown conditions, or uncertain developments; characterized by a lack of security or stability that threatens with danger.*

Precarious: *dependent on uncertain premises.*

Proactive: *acting in anticipation of future problems, needs, or changes.*

Prodromal: *a premonitory (giving warning) symptom of disease.*

Profound: *having intellectual depth and insight; difficult to fathom or understand; extending far below the surface.*

Recovery: *the process of combating a disorder (as alcoholism) or a real or perceived problem.*

Refute: *to prove wrong by argument or evidence: show to be false or erroneous; to deny the truth or accuracy of.*

Relevant: *having significant and demonstrable bearing on the matter at hand; affording evidence tending to prove or disprove the matter at issue or under discussion.*

Religion: *The discipline of God.*

Repertoire: *a supply of skills, devices, or expedients (part of the repertoire of a quarterback); broadly: amount, supply.*

Repugnant: *exciting distaste or aversion.*

Re-unification: *the act, process, or result of unifying: to make into a unit or a coherent whole: unite: the state of being unified.*

Sharing: *to partake of, use, experience, occupy, or enjoy with others; to have in common (they share a passion for opera); to grant or give a share in, often used with (shared the last of her water); to tell (as thoughts, feelings, or experiences) to others.*

Skeletal: *of, relating to, forming, attached to, or resembling a skeleton.*

Society: *a voluntary association of individuals for common ends; especially: an organized group working together or periodically meeting because of common interests, beliefs, or profession; an enduring and cooperating social group whose members have developed organized patterns of relationships through interac-*

tion with one another; a community, nation, or broad grouping of people having common traditions, institutions, and collective activities and interests.

Socio-: combining form; society: social.

Sociopathic: of, relating to, or characterized by asocial or antisocial behavior or exhibiting antisocial personality disorder.

Spirituality: relationship with God.

Sponsorship: one who assumes responsibility for some other person or thing; Introspect: a reflective looking inward: an examination of one's thoughts and feelings; Emphasis: special consideration of or stress or insistence on something; Ambiguity: uncertainty; Ideology: a manner of thinking characteristic of an individual, group, or culture; Scrutiny: a searching study, inquiry, or inspection: examination; a searching look; close watch: surveillance.

Substantiate: to establish by proof or competent evidence: verify.

Susceptibility: lack of ability to resist.

Tyranny: oppressive power.

Venue: locale; also: a place where events of a specific type are held.

Vernacular: of, relating to, or characteristic of a period, place, or group.

Viable: capable of working, functioning, or developing adequately; capable of existence and development as an independent unit; having a reasonable chance of succeeding.

Vortex: something that resembles a whirlpool; a mass of fluid with a whirling or circular motion that tends to form a cavity or vacuum in the center of the circle and to draw toward this cavity or vacuum bodies subject to its action.

NOTES

INDEX

Keith Simpson was born in Indiana on June 9, 1949. His family of origin is unknown. His adoption family taught him a code of moral conduct and responsibility, however knowing is not doing. Life is not always predictable, but change is inevitable. Time, experience and information sculpted the person writing this book. He embarked on this journey of discovery and change on May 5, 1982.

Keith's life, since 1992, has been focused on assisting others in the recovery process from substance abuse. He has been an alternative counselor to students found in violation of school substance rules and a transition advisor for the Arizona Department of Corrections.